Asia Bible Commentary Series

I0079323

JAMES

Langham

GLOBAL LIBRARY

Asia Bible Commentary Series

JAMES

Luke L. Cheung
and
Andrew B. Spurgeon

General Editor
Federico G. Villanueva

Old Testament Consulting Editors
Yohanna Katanacho, Tim Meadowcroft, Joseph Shao

New Testament Consulting Editors
Steve Chang, Andrew B. Spurgeon, Brian Wintle

© 2018 by Luke L. Cheung and Andrew B. Spurgeon

Published 2018 by Langham Global Library
An imprint of Langham Publishing
www.langhampublishing.org

Langham Publishing and its imprints are a ministry of Langham Partnership

Langham Partnership
PO Box 296, Carlisle, Cumbria, CA3 9WZ, UK
www.langham.org

Published in partnership with Asia Theological Association

ATA
QCC PO Box 1454 – 1154, Manila, Philippines
www.ataasia.com

ISBNs:
978-1-78368-866-1 Print
978-1-78368-549-3 ePub
978-1-78368-551-6 PDF

Luke L. Cheung and Andrew B. Spurgeon have asserted their right under the Copyright, Designs, and Patents Act, 1988 to be identified as the Author of this work.

All rights reserved. No part of this publication may be reproduced, stored in a retrieval system, or transmitted in any form or by any means, electronic, mechanical, photocopying, recording, or otherwise, without the prior written permission of the publisher or the Copyright Licensing Agency.

All Scripture quotations, unless otherwise indicated, are taken from the Holy Bible, New International Version®, NIV®. Copyright ©1973, 1978, 1984, 2011 by Biblica, Inc.™ Used by permission of Zondervan.

British Library Cataloguing in Publication Data
A catalogue record for this book is available from the British Library.

ISBN: 978-1-78368-866-1

Cover & Book Design: projectluz.com

Langham Partnership actively supports theological dialogue and an author's right to publish but does not necessarily endorse the views and opinions set forth and works referenced within this publication or guarantee its technical and grammatical correctness. Langham Partnership does not accept any responsibility or liability to persons or property as a consequence of the reading, use, or interpretation of its published content.

Drs Cheung and Spurgeon have given us a valuable resource that is both culturally sensitive and pastorally relevant. Their commentary of the Book of James is careful, comprehensive, and contextually relevant with many current examples from the Majority World. Readers looking for answers on issues like favoritism, controlling the tongue, and healing will find benefit from this very accessible commentary.

Rev Desmond Soh, DMin
Senior Director, Strategic Development,
Associate Professor of Practical Theology,
Singapore Bible College, Singapore

Luke Cheung and Andrew Spurgeon have given us a commentary on James that is outstanding. Erudite scholarship, relevant contextual application and a clear, engaging style brings the book of James alive to the Asian reader. Drawing upon insights from the text and its historical setting, the authors help the readers bridge the gap from biblical times to the present Asian context. Pastors, teachers and students of the Word will find plenty to chew on as they prepare to preach and teach in their local congregations and theological institutions. This is an indispensable book that must find a place in personal, church and institutional libraries.

Paul Cornelius, PhD
Regional Secretary (India), Asia Theological Association

Here you will find a fresh approach with new insights but also one that inter-acts with recent scholarship and applies the letter of James to Asian contexts. The style is very readable with insightful studies on pertinent Greek words that bring fuller meaning to the exhortations in the epistle without becoming overly technical. For example, the authors clarify that the Greek shows us that "trials are neutral; what matters is how we respond to them" (James 1:14–15). The volume is also full of insights on the book's structure, summary statements following each section, and many illustrations from Chinese sayings and other relevant passages in the Bible. You will love this book!

Rick Griffith, DMin
Director (English), Associate Professor of Biblical Studies,
Singapore Bible College, Singapore

To Helen Cheung
　　　—Luke L. Cheung

To Lori Spurgeon
　　　—Andrew B. Spurgeon

CONTENTS

Commentary

Topics

SERIES PREFACE

In recent years, we have witnessed one of the greatest shifts in the history of world Christianity. It used to be that the majority of Christians lived in the West, but Christians are now evenly distributed around the globe. This shift has implications for the task of interpreting the Bible from within our respective contexts, which is in line with the growing realization that every theology is contextual. Thus, the questions that we bring into our reading of the Bible will be shaped by our present realities as well as our historical and social locations. There is a need therefore to interpret the Bible for our own contexts.

The Asia Bible Commentary Series addresses this need. In line with the mission of the Asia Theological Association Publications, we have gathered evangelical Bible scholars working among Asians to write commentaries on each book of the Bible. The mission is to "produce resources that are biblical, pastoral, contextual, missional, and prophetic for pastors, Christian leaders, cross-cultural workers, and students in Asia." Although the Bible can be studied for different reasons, we believe that it is given primarily for the edification of the Body of Christ (2 Tim 3:16–17). The ABCS is designed to help pastors in their sermon preparation, cell group or lay leaders in their Bible study groups, and those training in seminaries or Bible schools.

Each commentary begins with an introduction that provides general information about the book's author and original context, summarizes the main message or theme of the book, and outlines its potential relevance to a particular Asian context. The introduction is followed by an exposition that combines exegesis and application. Here, we seek to speak to and empower Christians in Asia by using our own stories, parables, poems, and other cultural resources as we expound the Bible.

The Bible is actually Asian in that it comes from ancient West Asia, and there are many similarities between the world of the Bible and traditional Asian cultures. But there are also many differences that we need to explore in some depth. That is why the commentaries also include articles or topics in which we bring specific issues in Asian church, social, and religious contexts into dialogue with relevant issues in the Bible. We do not seek to resolve every tension that emerges but rather to allow the text to illumine the context and vice versa, acknowledging that we do not have all the answers to every mystery.

May the Holy Spirit, who inspired the writers of the Bible, bring light to the hearts and minds of all who use these materials, to the glory of God and to the building up of the churches!

Federico G. Villanueva
General Editor

AUTHORS' PREFACE

My Chinese commentary on James was published in 2008 and received the Tang Qing Christian Literature Award in the year after. In that same year, I was invited by Dr. Bruce Nicholls to write a commentary on James for the Asia Bible Commentary Series. Never would I have imagined that it would take another ten years to complete it!

I am grateful to Dr. Andrew B. Spurgeon, without whose aid this collaborative commentary on James would never have seen the light. Dr. Spurgeon has been most encouraging in this collaborative writing process, and I have found it a great learning experience to work with someone with rich multi-cultural understandings.

May this commentary be a blessing to those who long to be doers of God's word, and not just hearers (Jas 1:22). May God's name be magnified forever. Amen.

Luke L. Cheung
Vice-President,
Wilson Chow Professor,
China Graduate School of Theology

Every book has a history of composition – why it was written, how it came to be written, and who is to receive thanks. This book is no exception. It began in the minds of the ATA Publications Committee and the general editors of the Asia Bible Commentary Series, who invited Dr. Luke Cheung to write a commentary on James. He began the work, along with his wife, Helen, who contributed contextual applications. Part way through the writing, they invited me to join them as a co-author. So, I am grateful to Dr. and Mrs. Cheung for this opportunity, to Dr. Villanueva for accepting this change of plan, and to the ATA Publications Committee and Langham for their commitment to publishing commentaries that meet the needs of Christians in Asia.

The commentary was edited by Isobel Stevenson and her protégés, Karishma Paul and Tanya Ferdinandusz. I am thankful for their work in making sure that the commentary communicates the intent of the authors. I am also thankful to Bubbles Lactaoen, who made sure that the commentary followed the style guide, and Alex Lactaw, who diligently promotes the sales of the commentaries in the ABCS.

Several churches and friends in the USA support my wife's and my ministry in Asia. Their financial and prayer support enables us to teach, disciple, conduct seminars for pastors, and write books, including this book. So, I am extremely thankful for each of them, and for Global Outreach International, the mission agency that provides leadership and support for our work in Asia.

My parents gave me physical life and prayed for my spiritual life. When I surrendered to the Lord Jesus and gave my life to Christian service, they rejoiced. They have supported all my work, including the writing of commentaries. My mother went to be with the Lord as I worked on this commentary, leaving an unfillable gap in my soul. My dad, a major supporter of my ministries, reads my commentaries cover to cover. Thank you, dad, for your life, support, love, and prayers!

I am also thankful for my three sons, Ethan, Micah, and Jedidiah. They are my millennials who motivate me to keep on reading and explaining the Bible in terms of the way young Christians think and interact.

None has sacrificed as much as my dear wife, Lori. She patiently endured all the hours I spent away from her reading, writing, and rewriting. I owe special thanks to her. Without the freedom and encouragement she gives daily, I wouldn't be able to write even a page. Thank you, Lori.

Above all, I am thankful to God the Father and the Lord Jesus Christ who gave me eternal life and the joy of studying and explaining God's word.

Andrew B. Spurgeon
Professor of New Testament Studies,
School of Theology (English),
Singapore Bible College

LIST OF ABBREVIATIONS

BOOKS OF THE BIBLE

Old Testament

Gen, Exod, Lev, Num, Deut, Josh, Judg, Ruth, 1–2 Sam, 1–2 Kgs, 1–2 Chr, Ezra, Neh, Esth, Job, Ps/Pss, Prov, Eccl, Song, Isa, Jer, Lam, Ezek, Dan, Hos, Joel, Amos, Obad, Jonah, Mic, Nah, Hab, Zeph, Hag, Zech, Mal

New Testament

Matt, Mark, Luke, John, Acts, Rom, 1–2 Cor, Gal, Eph, Phil, Col, 1–2 Thess, 1–2 Tim, Titus, Phlm, Heb, Jas, 1–2 Pet, 1–2–3 John, Jude, Rev

BIBLE TEXTS AND VERSIONS

Divisions of the canon

NT	New Testament
OT	Old Testament

Ancient texts and versions

LXX	Septuagint
MT	Masoretic Text

Modern versions

ESV	English Standard Version
KJV	King James Version
NIV	New International Version
NJB	New Jerusalem Bible
NLT	New Living Translation
NRSV	New Revised Standard Version
TLV	Tree of Life Version

Journals, reference works, and series

AYBC	Anchor Yale Bible Commentaries

BDAG	*Greek-English Lexicon of the New Testament and Other Early Christian Literature*
BECNT	Baker Exegetical Commentary on the New Testament
BSac	*Bibliotheca Sacra*
ECB	Eerdmans Commentary on the Bible
EvQ	*Evangelical Quarterly*
HTR	*Harvard Theological Review*
ICC	International Critical Commentary
JETS	*Journal of the Evangelical Theological Society*
NICNT	New International Commentary on the New Testament
NIGTC	New International Greek Testament Commentary
NovT	*Novum Testamentum*
NTC	The New Testament in Context
NTS	*New Testament Studies*
NovTSup	Novum Testamentum Supplements
PNTC	Pillar New Testament Commentary
TDNT	Theological Dictionary of the New Testament
WBC	Word Bible Commentary
WUNT	*Wissenschaftliche Untersuchungen zum Neuen Testament*
ZECNT	Zondervan Exegetical Commentary on the New Testament

INTRODUCTION

In Hong Kong and China, criminals are often superstitiously religious. Ironically, both they and police officers worship the same folk god, Guan Gong, who represents righteousness! But their religiosity has no moral consequences – what both groups are seeking is protection from their opponents.

Unfortunately, some Asian Christians have a similar model of religiosity. They want God's blessings, but they do not want God to affect how they live. James will have none of this. He is convinced that our devotion to God must be reflected in the way we live, and so he writes a letter that is full of sound, practical advice. He speaks of how difficult it is to control our tongues, and how much we need to do so. He speaks against greed and envy, wrong desires, faith without substance, complaining, gossiping, and unfair labor practices. He gives wise advice about enduring suffering, knowing the source of temptation, having an authentic faith, praying for ailing believers, and restoring believers who are tempted to depart from the truth.

He also gives guidance on how to live in a situation of extreme socioeconomic disparity, such as still exists in Asia. Despite attempts to improve people's living conditions, factors such as globalization, technological advances, and market-oriented reform often cause further inequality and even polarization. Social and judicial systems are often biased against the poor, lower castes, indigenous people, and women. James speaks against oppressors and calls on those who have resources to care for those who lack them. This is a message that we as Christians still need to hear. We too must heed James's command to love and care for all.

Raymond Brown said that "the Book of James is one of the truly relevant sacred writings in the New Testament, meant for just such times as our own. It contains the counsel that will keep us . . . from sleeping through a revolution."[1] And Asia is indeed going through a revolution, not a political one but an economic and social and environmental revolution as we wrestle with economic growth, poverty elimination, climate change, social reform,

---

1. Raymond B. Brown, "Message of the Book of James for Today," *Review & Expositor* 66, no. 4 (1969): 415. Although Brown said this nearly five decades ago, it is still true today. Boyce in 2015 wrote, "[The book of James's] address is intensely personal as it offers a vision of a lifestyle and an ethic of faithfulness that promises to get us through the sometimes complex and painful realities of life. As such its collective impression has something of the character of 'reality therapy.'" James L. Boyce, "A Mirror of Identity: Implanted Word and Pure Religion in James 1:17–27," *Word & World* 35, no. 3 (2015): 214.

and equal opportunity in the workplace and in society. James's instructions can help Asian Christians address these issues with vibrancy and renewed commitment to the Lordship of Jesus Christ.

AUTHORSHIP

Who wrote James? The author identifies himself as "James" – but who is this James? In the NT, the name is used with reference to four different men:

- *James, the father of a disciple.* Jesus had two disciples named Judas, one of whom betrayed him. To avoid any confusion of the faithful Judas with Judas Iscariot, the former is identified as "Judas the son of James" (Luke 6:16; Acts 1:13).
- *James, the son of Alphaeus, a disciple.* Jesus also had two disciples named James. We know very little about the one known as James the son of Alphaeus (Matt 10:3; Mark 3:18; Luke 6:15; Acts 1:13).
- *James, the son of Zebedee, a disciple.* This James and his brother John were part of the inner circle of three disciples (Peter being the other) who were with Jesus on the Mount of Transfiguration and on other special occasions (Matt 17:1–8; Mark 5:37, 13:3; Luke 9:28–36).
- *James, the brother of Jesus.* Jesus had a half-brother or stepbrother called James (Matt 13:55; Mark 6:3) who did not accompany him during his earthly ministry. It seems that this James later had a special revelation of the Lord that appointed him an apostle, prepared him for ministry, and gave him a special position of leadership in the Jerusalem church (Acts 15:13–29; 1 Cor 15:7).

Any of the above men could have written the letter of James, but given that we know so little about the first two, they are unlikely candidates. At first glance, James the son of Zebedee seems to be the best candidate: He was a disciple, he was in the inner circle of three disciples, he was at the Lord's transfiguration, he had witnessed the Lord's resurrection, and he had worked with John and Peter in establishing the early church in Jerusalem. But his execution by Herod Agrippa to curry favor with the Jews (Acts 12:2) probably occurred before this letter was written.

The most likely author of this letter is thus James the son of Joseph and brother of Jesus. He was regarded as one of the pillars of the church in Jerusalem (Gal 2:9) and presided over the Jerusalem Council, which met when some Jewish Christians tried to insist that Gentiles could not be Christians unless they accepted circumcision and obeyed the law of Moses (Acts 15). James's lineage (like Jesus, he was a son of David), his close association with the Lord Jesus (his half-brother or stepbrother), and his being a witness to the resurrection (1 Cor 15:7) would have given him the credentials to be a leader of the Jewish Christians to whom he addressed this letter.

Some scholars have challenged this view. They give four reasons for doing so.[2] First, they claim that the style and vocabulary of the letter are too polished to have come from a Jewish peasant. To illustrate the literary quality of James, they point to the Greek philosophical and religious phrase "the cycle of nature" used in James 3:6. But James could have come across this type of language in Jewish writings that reflect Greek influence (e.g., the works of Philo). Also, we may be underestimating the level of literacy of Galilean Jews.[3] Finally, ancient scholars often used an amanuensis (a scribe) to write down their thoughts. Paul, for example, used an amanuensis named Tertius to write his letter to the Romans (Rom 16:22). James, too, could have dictated this letter to a scribe who polished his Greek.

The second objection to James's authorship is that the letter is not distinctively Christian; it could have been written by a non-Christian Jew. For example, the letter never mentions Christ's resurrection or the Holy Spirit. The name Jesus Christ appears only twice (1:1; 2:1), and if these two references were omitted, there would be nothing to show that this was a Christian book. But the nature of the recipients can influence the nature of the letter. Paul, writing to Gentiles, needed to address outright Christian themes. James was writing to Jews who had accepted that Jesus was the risen Messiah but needed practical advice on how the law of Moses applied in their new Christian lives. This was a theme that Jesus had preached on in the Sermon on the Mount, and James's teaching mirrors that of his brother.

The third objection to James's authorship is closely linked to the second: This letter includes too many Jewish elements that were discarded in early

---

2. Blomberg and Kamell engage with these arguments in detail in Craig L. Blomberg and Mariam J. Kamell, *James*. ZECNT, ed. Clinton E. Arnold (Grand Rapids: Zondervan, 2008), 21–36.

3. The following authors argue that the level of literacy among the peasants in the first century is underrated: J. N. Sevenster, *Do You Know Greek: How Much Greek Could the First Jewish Christian Have Known?* NovTSup 19 (Leiden: Brill, 1968), 96–175, 190–191; Stanley E. Porter, "Jesus and the Use of Greek in Galilee," in *Studying the Historical Jesus: Evaluations of the State of Current Research*, ed. B. Chilton and Craig A. Evans (Leiden: Brill, 1994), 128–147; Sean Freyne, *Galilee: From Alexander the Great to Hadrian 323 BCE to 135 CE: A Study of Second Temple Judaism* (Edinburgh: T & T Clark, 1998), 139–145.

Christianity. For example, the author refers to the law of Moses as "the law of liberty" and "the royal law" (1:25; 2:8, 12), whereas Paul speaks of it as "the law of sin and death" (Rom 8:2). Nor is there any sign of tension about religious matters such as circumcision or what food may or may not be eaten (contrast Gal 2:11–13; Acts 21:20–25). But, once again, we need to remember that James was writing to Jews among whom there were no conflicts about the status of the law. Tensions over cultural practices such as Sabbath-keeping or kosher food laws were not an issue for his audience – they kept the Sabbath and ate kosher food. Paul had to address these issues because his letters were addressed to both Jews and Gentiles (see Gal 2:11–14). For James's readers, the law was still a valuable guide to practical living.[4]

The fourth objection to James's authorship is that this book was not imme-diately accepted as part of the NT canon. Although that is true, no one denies that the early church valued this book enough to preserve it. Furthermore, the objections to this book's inclusion in the canon came mainly from the Western church, and particularly after the Reformation. At that time, some interpreters mistakenly thought that James contradicted Paul's teachings on justification by faith. It seems likely that the doubts about this book reflect the church's failure to acknowledge its Jewish roots.

In summary, none of these arguments are sufficient to deny that a Jewish Christian named James wrote this letter to a primarily Jewish audience. Most likely, this James was the brother of Jesus, as has been believed since the days of the church fathers.

DATE OF COMPOSITION

If James the brother of our Lord was the writer of this letter, it must have been written before AD 62, the year in which James died as a martyr.[5] Since the letter does not mention the tensions about the place of Gentiles in the church, the controversy over circumcision or the decisions of the Jerusalem Council (Acts 15:13–29), it is likely that it was written before AD 49, when the council met. Some scholars argue that the references to caring for the poor and paying workers their wages (2:1–7, 15–16; 5:1–6) reflect conditions at the time of the great famine that occurred in Judea in AD 46 (Acts 11:28). If

4. Douglas J. Moo, *The Letter of James*, PNTC (Grand Rapids: Eerdmans, 2000), 15.
5. Flavius Josephus, *Antiquities of the Jews*, XX.9. For more on James's birth, ministry, and death, see Dan G. McCartney, *James*, BECNT (Grand Rapids: Baker Academic, 2009), 9–31.

so, James could have written this letter in the mid-40s, making it one of the earliest writings in the NT.

RECIPIENTS

James wrote his letter "to the twelve tribes scattered among the nations" (1:1). The "twelve tribes" were the descendants of the twelve sons of Jacob (who was given the name "Israel"). So "the twelve tribes" was a way of referring to the entire Jewish nation. James was thus writing specifically to Jewish Christians.[6] In this, he differs from Paul, whose letters were addressed to both Jewish and Gentile Christians.

Further, James was writing to Jewish Christians who were "scattered among the nations." This phrase translates one word (*diaspora*), which is sometimes translated as "in the Dispersion" (ESV). This group certainly included Jewish Christians who had been scattered by the persecution that arose after the death of Stephen (Acts 8:1–4).[7] But it would also have included all the Jews who had fled the land of Israel at various times and settled elsewhere, sometimes for many generations.[8] Some of these Jews had accepted Jesus as the Messiah, and James was confident that their numbers would grow as more and more Jews acknowledged Jesus. The Apostle Peter, writing to a similar group of Jewish Christians, listed their locations as "Pontus, Galatia, Cappadocia, Asia, and Bithynia" (1 Pet 1:1), all parts of what is now Turkey.

Today there are millions of people who have been scattered from places like Syria, Afghanistan, and Myanmar. They have had to leave their homes and flee to safety. Imagine how they would rejoice if they received a message from their homeland! Similarly, the Jewish Christians scattered across Asia Minor would have been glad to receive James's exhortations. His letter from Jerusalem

---

6. There may, of course, have been a few Gentile Christians who worshiped with these Jewish congregations, but they would have been in the minority. For more on the intended recipients, see Blomberg and Kamell, 32–35.

7. O. S. Hawkins, "Preaching from the Book of James," *Southwestern Journal of Theology* 43, no. 1 (2000): 56–57; see also Arthur James, "James," in *South Asia Bible Commentary* (Udaipur, India: Open Door Publications, 2015), 1732.

8. For the view that the addressees were Jewish Christians (the two tribes of Judah and Benjamin) and Gentiles (representing the ten tribes of Israel who fled Judea after the Assyrian invasion), see Joel Marcus, "'The Twelve Tribes in the Diaspora' (James 1.1)," *NTS* 60, no. 4 (2014): 433–447.

would have strengthened the strong but invisible connection between the *diaspora* communities and the motherland.[9]

PURPOSE OF THE LETTER

James's teachings follow the pattern of Wisdom literature, and so are similar to the teaching found in books like Proverbs, Ecclesiastes, and Job. Wisdom literature is full of "short ethical instructions . . . giving practical advice for one's life."[10] James wants the Jewish Christians to live wisely, and so he writes this letter to help them exercise their faith practically in a hostile world.

But James was not only influenced by OT models. His teachings are so similar to the Sermon on the Mount that one scholar says that James "has made the wisdom of Jesus his own and re-expresses it in new formulations of his own."[11]

The Jewish Christians James was writing to lived in a world that persecuted them for their faith (1:2–4).[12] Such persecution resulted in socioeconomic disparities that brought tensions within the community. For example, wealthy people took poor people to court (2:1–7), oppressed the marginalized (4:13–5:6), and exploited day laborers (5:1–6). Meanwhile the poor lacked adequate food and clothing (2:15). Some within the congregation, both rich and poor, lashed out with uncontrolled speech (2:9–12; 4:11) and started fights and divisions within the community (3:13–16; 4:1–4). There was even inappropriate behavior when the congregation gathered for worship or to settle legal disputes, with the wealthy receiving preferential treatment while the poor were insulted (2:3).

James explains that all these types of behavior spring from evil desires and from outside influences and the devil (1:13–15; 3:14–16; 4:1–4, 7). Christians can, however, change their behavior by obeying the "law of freedom" which brings moral and spiritual maturity (1:25; 2:12). This law frees Christians to love God (1:12; 2:5, 23) and their neighbors (2:8) because it frees them from the power of evil desires (1:14–15; 4:1–3). Instead of fighting for limited

---

9. So argues Richard J. Bauckham, "James, 1 Peter, Jude and 2 Peter," in *A Vision for the Church*, ed. M. Bockmuehl and M. B. Thompson (Edinburgh: T & T Clark, 1997), 154.
10. Patrick J. Hartin, "'Come Now, You Rich, Weep and Wail . . .' (James 5:1–6)." *Journal of Theology for Southern Africa* 84 (1993): 57.
11. Richard J. Bauckham, *James*, in ECB, ed. James D. G. Dunn (Grand Rapids: Eerdmans, 2003), 1484.
12. For an article on the theology of suffering (*Leidenstheologie*) as the primary focus of James, see Peter H. Davids, "Theological Perspectives on the Epistle of James," *JETS* 23, no. 2 (1980): 97–103.

goods, Christians should share what they have. Their faith should show itself in actions (2:14–26).

James regards faith that shows itself in action as a sign of Christian maturity. Mature Christians love God, obey God's laws, and love their neighbor (2:8). Such maturity originates from God, who has given the word of truth and wisdom from above to his people (1:18; 3:17–18). God's grace and mercy empower Christians to live in a godly and mature way in a difficult and oppressive society (4:6; 5:11).

We, too, live in a hostile world in which Christians are persecuted and killed.[13] Even if Christians are not physically persecuted, they may still experience other forms of discrimination. For example, employers may bypass Christians and offer promotions to less qualified employees.

How do we prepare Christians to live in a world where they are persecuted and where evils like bonded labor, the exploitation of women and children, and organ harvesting are rife? James says that we do it by teaching Christians God's wisdom. If they follow God's law of liberty, they can live in the way that the ancient Confucian scholar Mencius endorsed when he said, "Looking up, feeling no shame before the heaven. Looking down, feeling no regret before people." That saying captures the heart of what James says in this letter: Look to God for wisdom on how to love our fellow human beings.

OUTLINE

Because James is writing this letter in the style of Wisdom literature, he does not present his argument in the linear style that Paul does. Instead, he uses a circular style, in which he returns to the same topic repeatedly at different points in the letter (e.g., he speaks about the rich in 1:10–11; 2:5–6 and 5:1, and warns against sins of speech in 3:3–12; 4:11; 5:9).[14]

1:1 Greetings
    1:1a The Author of the Letter
    1:1b The Recipients of the Letter

---

13. *The Voice of the Martyrs* gives regular updates on these events (https://www.persecution.com).
14. For a detailed outline with exegetical ideas, see George B. Davis, "Preaching from the Book of James," *Criswell Theological Review* 1 (1986): 137–147. For the structure of early letters and how James fits within it, see Fred O. Francis, "Form and Function of the Opening and Closing Paragraphs of James and 1 John," *Zeitschrift Für Die Neutestamentliche Wissenschaft Und Die Kunde Der Älteren Kirche* 61, nos. 1–2 (1970): 110–126. See also Luke L. Cheung, *The Genre, Composition and Hermeneutics of James* (Carlisle: Paternoster, 2003).

JAMES 1:1

GREETINGS

Nowadays, formal letter-writing ("snail mail") has given way to informal emails, texts, and tweets. But in the ancient world, letter-writing was an art. Each letter began by introducing the author(s), and naming the addressee(s), and greeting them (see, for example, Acts 15:23; 23:26). This greeting might be followed by a blessing on the recipient(s) of the letter and thanksgiving.

James follows that simple but efficient pattern:

> James, a servant of God and of the Lord Jesus Christ
> To the twelve tribes scattered among the nations:
> Greetings. (1:1)

James identifies himself as the author (with a description of his role), identifies the addressees, and greets them. Unlike Paul, he does not include a blessing (Phil 1:2) or a prayer of thanksgiving (Phil 1:3–11).

1:1A THE AUTHOR OF THE LETTER

Although he was probably not a disciple during Jesus's earthly ministry, James was active in the church in Jerusalem as early as AD 36 (three to six years after the Lord's resurrection). That is why Paul made a trip to Jerusalem to meet him and Cephas and give a report of his ministry (Gal 1:18–19). Eight years later, in AD 44, when Peter (the greatest of the apostles) was forced to flee Jerusalem, he handed James the leadership of the church there. James was one of the three pillars of that church, along with Peter and John (Gal 2:9). In AD 49, when delegates from the church in Antioch came to Jerusalem to discuss the Gentiles' inclusion in the people of God without being circumcised, James chaired the Council of Jerusalem and issued the decisive apostolic decree (Acts 15:13–29). Citing the words of his ancestor David, he authorized the inclusion of the Gentiles in the churches worldwide. That decree went out to all the churches in Antioch, Syria, and Cilicia, and it changed history.

Eight years later (AD 57), when some people challenged Paul's faithfulness to Judaism, James advised him to demonstrate his commitment to the law in a practical way by fulfiling the requirements associated with a Nazirite vow (Acts 21:18–25). Paul's obedience to James's instruction indicates that James was indeed in a position of leadership. It is thus not surprising that the ancient Christian historian Eusebius (AD 260–339) referred to James as the first bishop of Jerusalem.[1]

Given his prominent position in the church, it is surprising that James describes himself as merely "a servant" (1:1a).[2] The word translated "servant" (*doulos*) can also be translated as "slave" (e.g., Col 3:22; Titus 2:9). Servants and slaves had very low social standing. By adopting this title, James and the other apostles were acknowledging their call to humiliation. Paul even wrote, "It seems to me that God has put us apostles on display at the end of the procession, like those condemned to die in the arena. We have been made a spectacle to the whole universe, to angels as well as to human beings" (1 Cor 4:9).

James's humble introduction of himself is all the more striking in these days of celebrity culture, when people are eager to post selfies showing that they have been close to someone famous. James could easily have boasted that he grew up alongside Jesus (Mark 6:2–3; 3:31–34; John 7:3–5). Instead, he humbly referred to himself as Jesus's slave. His example also speaks to those of us who overvalue titles, honors, degrees, prestige, a name, heritage, and lineage. What really matters is how we see ourselves in the sight of God and before the people we serve. Like James, we are called to be "servants" or "slaves" to God and the Lord Jesus Christ, and to the sheep we shepherd. Christian leadership is servanthood – just as the Lord Jesus Christ himself taught when he washed his disciples' feet.

Yet the title "servant of God" is also a term of honor. In the OT, this title was used of Moses (Deut 34:5; Dan 9:11), Joshua (Judg 2:8) and David (2 Sam 7:8; Jer 33:21; Ezek 37:25), and of prophets like Amos (Amos 3:7), Jeremiah (Jer 7:25), Ezekiel (Ezek 38:17), and Daniel (Dan 9:10). These men were servants of God because they were chosen by God and authorized to be his representatives.[3] To be God's servant was to represent him faithfully.

James then explains whose servant he is: "A servant of God and of the Lord Jesus Christ." This combination is striking, for no religious Jew would ever speak of God as being on an equal footing with a man. Clearly, James is implying that Jesus has a unique status. This point is underlined when we spot James's allusion to the OT phase "the servant of the LORD" and note that he speaks of the *Lord* Jesus Christ. James is giving YHWH and the Lord Jesus

---

1. Eusebius, *Ecclesiastical History* 2.1.2–3; 4.5.3–4; 5.12.1–2; compare 2.23.4–7.
2. The apostle Paul describes himself in the same terms (Rom 1:1; Gal 1:10; Phil 1:1; Titus 1:1).
3. David E. Garland, "Severe Trials, Good Gifts, and Pure Religion: James 1," *Review & Expositor* 83, no. 3 (1986): 383.

Christ the same status and saying that he is the servant of both, submitting to their authority and obeying their commands.

In calling Jesus "Lord" here and in 2:1, James is acknowledging that Jesus is the Messiah (a Jewish title that is translated "Christ" in Greek). The Jews of the time thought that the Messiah would be a Jewish king descended from David who would be God's representative on earth, one whom God would refer to as "my son" (Pss 2; 110). They were prepared to hail such a human king as their human lord. But the Christians recognized that the Messiah was not just God's representative but his incarnation on earth. Peter openly proclaimed this on the Day of Pentecost: "God has made this Jesus, whom you crucified, both Lord and Christ" (Acts 2:36). Here the word translated "Lord" is the same one used to refer to God in the Greek translation of the OT. Jesus was a descendant of King David and the ruler of a kingdom far greater than that of any earthly king, for he was equal to God, the Lord.

1:1B THE RECIPIENTS OF THE LETTER

After introducing himself, James states whom he is writing to: "the twelve tribes scattered among the nations" (1:1b). By identifying them as *the twelve tribes*, he was reminding them of a key element in their identity – their hope that one day the twelve tribes of Israel would be reunited. This hope had been nurtured since the Assyrian and Babylonian exiles (722 BC and 586 BC).[4] The exilic and post-exilic prophets had promised a future restoration of the nation (see Isa 49:6; 54:7; 56:8; Jer 31:8–14; Zech 10:6–12). Ezekiel had prophesied that one day the ten tribes of Israel and the two tribes of Judah would be reunited with David as their king, and God would dwell among them (Ezek 37:15–28). So, when James addressed those he was writing to as "the twelve tribes" and referred to himself as "a servant of God . . . and *Christ*" [Messiah], he was evoking familiar imagery of God actively restoring his people to their former glory.

James continues with this imagery as he addresses them as those "scattered among the nations." The Greek word *diaspora*, which the NIV translates as "scattered among the nations," was a technical term referring to the literal dispersion of Israel outside of Palestine. It is the word that the ancient Greek version of the OT (the Septuagint) used to translate verses like Deuteronomy 30:4 that refer to the Lord bringing back his scattered people to their land (see

---

4. Marcus, "'The Twelve Tribes in the Diaspora' (James 1.1)," 433–447.

also Ps 147:2; Neh 1:9; Isa 49:6; Jer 15:7; 41:17; Dan 12:2). By using this term, James reminds the scattered Jewish Christians of the promise of future restoration. The Lord Jesus, their Messiah (Christ), is assuring them through his servant James that they can continue to hope for future restoration. They are the firstfruit, but a full harvest will follow.

These believers did not yet call themselves "Christians," for that was the name that their opponents used to ridicule them (Acts 11:26; 1 Pet 4:16). In fact, they probably did not think of themselves as anything more than Jews whose messianic hopes had been fulfilled in the coming of the Lord Jesus. They understood that he would restore the whole of Israel and that the nations would be included in this restoration. Jesus's choosing of twelve disciples, representing the twelve tribes of Israel, was regarded as a sign that God's redemption would extend to all the Jews. So although James writes to "those Jews who already confess the Messiah Jesus," his message is actually addressed "to all Israel."[5] It challenges God's people to live as renewed people in a corrupt world. A new age is dawning!

But if James was writing only to Jewish Christians in Asia Minor, why should we who live in Asia and are not Jewish read this letter? We should read it because the Messiah's kingdom includes Gentiles (Acts 15:16–19), and the principles James lays out apply equally to Jews and Gentiles. James explains them in ways that Jewish readers would understand best, but his practical instructions and wisdom are just as applicable to us as they were to them and heeding his words will bring us blessings (1:23–25).

---

5. Richard J. Bauckham, "James, 1 Peter, Jude and 2 Peter," in *A Vision for the Church*, eds. M. Bockmuehl and M. B. Thompson (Edinburgh: T & T Clark, 1997), 154.

JAMES 1:2–27

PROLOGUE: SPIRITUAL MATURITY

When a Jewish teacher of the law asked Jesus to name the greatest commandment, he replied by listing two commandments: "Hear, O Israel: The Lord our God, the Lord is one. Love the Lord your God with all your heart and with all your soul and with all your mind and with all your strength" and "Love your neighbor as yourself" (Mark 12:29–31).

Since these commandments were at the heart of the Jewish law (the Torah), James's Jewish readers would have known them, and they would have recognized his subtle reference to them in this long prologue in which he spells out the principles that he will expand on later in the letter. Such prologues were common in the Jewish Wisdom tradition. For example, the book of Proverbs also begins with a prologue that explains how to listen to what is said in the book.

Perfect obedience to these two commandments – love God and love your neighbors – would mark the readers as spiritually mature, or "perfect." James wants his readers to settle for nothing less. So he begins by explaining how believers should perfectly love the perfect God (1:2–18). Then, he explains how believers must live in obedience to God's perfect law, which commands them to perfectly love their neighbors (1:19–27).

Following the pattern of Jesus himself, James stresses the broad ethical implications of God's law. For example, Jesus did not see the commandment against murder as applying only to killing but extended it to apply to the anger and insults that lead to violence and murder (Matt 5:21–22). For both Jesus and James, the practical outworking of obeying God is demonstrated in the details of daily living. This means that as we study God's word, we must think deeply about how what we read should shape all aspects of our lives.

Our study of the book of James should thus challenge us to live with godliness and maturity, obeying God and loving his people. As we learn to do this, we will start walking on the path to perfection and will be imitating our Father who is perfect.

1:2–18 PERFECT LOVE FOR GOD

Every culture has phrases that people from that culture readily understand while outsiders are clueless. In the English-speaking world, for example, if someone says, "look at that Romeo and Juliet," he is referring to a couple who are very much in love. In India, if a group calls for a nationwide "bandh," they want all institutions and businesses to be closed for a day or two. In Singapore, a "chope" is an object placed beside a seat to show that someone is sitting there.

The Jews, too, had unique expressions that conveyed a whole set of meanings. *Shema* ("hear" or "listen") was such a term. It is the first word in the verse that sums up the faith of Israel: "Hear [*shema*], O Israel: The LORD our God, the LORD is one. Love the LORD your God with all your heart and with all your soul and with all your strength" (Deut 6:4–5). These words were regularly repeated in Jewish worship. So the word "Shema" came to be shorthand for the Jewish confession of faith, which laid down two key principles. The first was that Israel's God, YHWH, was unique. He was "one of a kind," and thus Israel should worship him alone and not the many gods of the surrounding cultures. The second principle related to how Israel was to worship God – they were to love him with all their heart, soul, and strength.

James does not mention the Shema in so many words in this letter. But his Jewish audience knew it and would probably have recognized that in 1:2–18 he is focusing on the second part of the Shema and on what it means to love God perfectly with all one's heart, soul, and strength. One grows toward this type of spiritual maturity as one learns to handle trials and doubts, as well as riches and possessions.

1:2–12 Loving God

James wants his readers to love God with all their hearts by submitting all their desires to him (1:5–8); he wants them to love God with all their souls by being willing to give up their lives for him (1:2–4); and he wants them to love God with all their strength by seeing all that they possess or do not possess as coming from him (1:9–11).

1:2–4 Loving God with all your soul/life
Suffering was common among the early Christians. They endured hostility from their families, from religious and political authorities, and from those whose income was disrupted when people ceased to worship pagan gods. James and his fellow Christians in Jerusalem had witnessed the stoning of Stephen and the execution of James the son of Zebedee, and had suffered at the hands of men like Saul (Acts 6:8–7:60; 8:1; 9:1–2; 12:1–2). So James can identify with

the suffering of those he repeatedly addresses as his "brothers and sisters."[1] He is not writing to suffering people as someone who has never suffered himself. He has shared their trials. James must also have been familiar with the ordinary trials of life including poor health, poverty, and death.

That being the case, a reader may be puzzled by James's opening words to the suffering Christians: "Consider it pure joy . . . whenever you face trials of many kinds" (1:2). How can James possibly tell someone to consider it a *joy* when they or members of their family are enduring suffering or persecution?

The answer lies in the exact phrasing James uses. A literal translation of the Greek would read "All joy count it," which could be paraphrased as "count every happiness when you endure trials" (1:2b).[2] James wants his readers to focus on the happiness that is to come and on their happiness in the past as they go through trials. On the one hand, they are to be like a woman enduring the severe pain of giving birth while rejoicing that a new life, one that will bring great joy, is coming into the world. The woman does not rejoice in the pain as such, but she rejoices in the coming child. On the other hand, believers can also look back on past happiness. James is telling them to "count all the happiness your family brought you over the past twenty years; your persecutors can't take that away from you." He does not want them to focus on their sufferings but on their joys. He would have approved of the words of the old hymn, "Count your many blessings, name them one by one, and it will surprise you what the Lord has done."[3] When believers face trials, James wants them to count their blessings.

Christians in Asia should also adopt this attitude. Trials are as much a part of our lives as blessings. Rather than focusing on the trials, we should focus on God's blessings. Job's answer to his wife illustrates the type of attitude James wants us to have: "Shall we accept good from God, and not trouble?" (Job 2:10).

Trials will certainly come, for the word "whenever" implies that they are inevitable. They may take the form of persecution (2:7), poverty (2:6–7; 5:1–6), sickness (5:14), or something else. They will be "of many kinds" and

---

1. See 1:2, 16, 19; 2:1, 5, 14; 3:1, 10, 12; 4:11; 5:7, 9, 10, 12, 19. Although the Greek text only has "brothers" (as reflected in the KJV), the translation, "brothers and sisters" is appropriate since this letter is written to both men and women.
2. James's Greek is interesting here: The word "greetings" (*charein*) is closely followed by the word "joy" (*charan*), a word that sounds very similar to *charein*. In the next few words, he uses alliteration: *peirasmois peripesēte poikilois* (literally, "trials face many"). There are many similar examples of his eloquence in the rest of the letter.
3. Johnson Oatman, "When upon life's billows you are tempest tossed," 1897.

will be different from person to person, from time to time, from event to event. James does not speculate on the source of these trials. He simply acknowledges that they are part of life. No one is exempt from the trials that come on individuals and communities. It is by enduring trials that Christians prove the genuineness of their faith. Job is the classic example of this, for his response to trials proved that he trusted God (5:11).

The reason James gives for enduring trials is "because you know that the testing of your faith produces perseverance" (1:3). A Chinese proverb says, "Steel is refined by fire, and knife is sharpened by stone." In the same way trials refine and strengthen those who endure them. They develop perseverance. The Greek word translated "perseverance" could also be translated "endurance" or "steadfastness." It literally means the ability to *remain under*, that is, the ability to hold a position and keep on doing something while enduring pain or strain, without weakening or trying to escape. This is not a passive attitude, but an active one. It is not just putting up with things, but rather a determination to stand one's ground. It is the attitude of a soldier staying at his post and refusing to retreat in a fierce battle, or of a farmer who loses one crop to drought or some other disaster, but persists and plants again the following year (see 5:7). Endurance shows one's determination to persist in faith, refusing to back down, and overcoming anxiety, fear, and insecurity.

Perseverance in trials brings benefits: "Let perseverance finish its work so that you may be mature and complete, not lacking anything" (1:4; see also 1 Thess 5:23). The word translated "mature" is *teleios*, which comes from the root *telos* meaning "purpose" or "goal."[4] Trials are not an end in themselves, nor is perseverance good for its own sake; both serve the purpose of bringing a person to a state of spiritual maturity. The final goal is perfection in character, being mature, holy, and righteous in the eyes of God. A person gains maturity by enduring trials, strengthened by the memory of past happiness, and by the knowledge that suffering serves a purpose.

This is a difficult but creative way to look at the trials that are common to everyone. We cannot choose *not* to face them, but we can choose *how* to face them. Christians have no need to detach themselves from the emotions that are the source of pain; neither do they need to resort to charms, incantations, Feng Shui, offerings to gods, or even witchcraft, when misfortune comes. Instead, we are to face hardship with faith and steadfastness, refusing

---

4. *Teleios* (meaning "goal" or "perfect") is also used in James 1:17, 1:25, and 3:2. It is a synonym of the word *holoklēroi*, "complete." When used together, as in 1:4, the words reinforce each other and could be translated as "perfectly perfect," on in other words, "not lacking anything."

to succumb to negative feelings and reactions, and knowing that trials bring perseverance. James himself is our example for he was martyred a few years after writing this letter.

So, are we going to endure our suffering with a fatalistic attitude? Or are we going to count our blessings and endure trials knowing that they are tools to refine us and bring us to spiritual maturity? James encourages us to rejoice in God's goal for us – he wants us to become people of integrity, perfect in character, mature, holy, and righteous. While we are not yet perfect, we should be moving along the path toward the perfect maturity that will be ours when the Lord returns.[5] As the great Confucian scholar Mencius said, "whenever Heaven invests a person with great responsibilities, it first tries their resolve, exhausts their muscles and bones, starves their body, leaves them destitute, and confronts their every endeavor. In this way, their patience and endurance are developed and their weaknesses are overcome."[6]

Trials and suffering reveal our inner disposition, our faith in God, and our faithfulness to him. Sufferings are thus invitations for us to evaluate our relationship with God. They are moments of truth, opening up new horizons of experience and placing before us challenges that can take us a step forward. Trials are like checkpoints in our life journeys, enabling us to see whether we are really on the right track to perfection. They are often the most effective teachers for those who wish to learn maturity.

We are not to sadistically desire pain, but are to persevere, counting our joys and trusting that the outcome of our trials will be good, just as a mother endures birth pains in order to bear a child. The challenge for us is to remain focused on our past blessings and the end result of suffering: Christian maturity.[7]

In all this, the Lord Jesus is our finest example: "And being found in appearance as a man, he humbled himself by becoming obedient to death – even death on a cross! Therefore, God exalted him to the highest place and gave him the name that is above every name" (Phil 2:8–9). The Apostle Peter reminds us of the Lord's attitude when he suffered: "When they hurled their insults at him, he did not retaliate; when he suffered, he made no threats. Instead, he

---

5. Ralph P. Martin, *James*, WBC (Waco: Word, 1988), 17; Dale C. Allison, *James*, International Critical Commentary (London: Bloomsbury, 2013), 159–160.
6. David Hinton, *Mencius* (Washington, DC: Counterpoint, 1998), 230.
7. For more on the concept of perfection through suffering, see Patrick J. Hartin, "Call to Be Perfect through Suffering (James 1:2-4): The Concept of Perfection in the Epistle of James and the Sermon on the Mount," *Biblica* 77, no. 4 (1996): 477–492.

entrusted himself to him who judges justly" (1 Pet 2:23). James is encouraging believers to have a similar attitude.

The church in China has set a great example of suffering and perseverance through trials and persecutions. During the Cultural Revolution (1966–76), Christians around the world feared that none of the Christians in China would survive. To their surprise, persecution did not extinguish the church in China; instead, churches thrived. Many who died under persecution did so without renouncing their faith in Jesus Christ. Those who survived, lived authentically and spread the gospel so faithfully behind the Bamboo Curtain that churches in China are vibrant to this day.

Huang Ming Dao, a prominent Chinese Christian leader, has told how he was tempted to renounce his Christian faith when persecution struck. Nevertheless, he endured twenty-three years of imprisonment (1956–79).[8] His faithfulness in prison and his testimony when released encouraged others to endure persecution. His steadfastness in Christ continues to speak to Chinese churches even after his death in 1991.

When Christians endure trials, counting their past blessings and looking to the maturity endurance brings, they are like steel that has been refined by fire or a knife that has been sharpened by a stone. As Peter says, "In all this you greatly rejoice, though now for a little while you may have had to suffer grief in all kinds of trials. These have come so that the proven genuineness of your faith – of greater worth than gold, which perishes even though refined by fire – may result in praise, glory and honor when Jesus Christ is revealed" (1 Pet 1:6–7).

1:5–8 Loving God with all your heart/mind

When people face repeated trials, they can feel overwhelmed, leading to feelings of discouragement and inadequacy. They find it hard to love God with all their soul, as James has been advising them to do. How can they love God with all their heart in such circumstances? Doing so seems to require more wisdom than they possess.

To those in such situations, James offers advice that sounds as if it could have come from the book of Proverbs: "If any of you lacks wisdom, you should ask God, who gives generously to all without finding fault, and it will be given to you" (1:5). The "wisdom" he is referring to is much more than just knowledge or the type of information you can get on the Internet. Wisdom

---

8. Leslie Lyall, *Three of China's Mighty Men* (London: OMF Books, 1973).

involves the ability to live wisely, knowing the difference between good and evil, and choosing to do what is good.

Solomon's life and reign illustrate what wisdom is. The Lord appeared to Solomon, saying, "ask for whatever you want me to give you" (1 Kgs 3:5). Solomon answered: "Now, Lord my God, you have made your servant king in place of my father David. But I am only a little child and do not know how to carry out my duties . . . So give your servant a discerning heart to govern your people and to distinguish between right and wrong" (1 Kgs 3:7, 9). The Lord answered his request and gave him "a wise and discerning heart" (1 Kgs 3:12). Solomon then demonstrated his wisdom in the way he handled a dispute between two prostitutes involving a dead and a living child (1 Kgs 3:16–28). Wisdom is more than knowledge; it is skill in living.

Everyone needs wisdom to navigate life. Jesus declared that his followers would be in need of wisdom when he said, "I am sending you out like sheep among wolves. Therefore be as shrewd as snakes and as innocent as doves" (Matt 10:16). How can one learn such shrewdness or wisdom? James's answer is, "You should ask God for it" (1:5). The tense of the Greek verb used here implies that this is not a one-time request. As we repeatedly face trials, we need to repeatedly ask God for wisdom.

How can we keep on asking God for the same thing? We can do so because God gives wisdom generously (as he did to Solomon) and "without finding fault" or "without a second thought."[9] He does not complain or scold, as *we* sometimes do, "I gave you wisdom last week, why do you need it again? What have you done with the last bit of wisdom I gave you?" Our God does not grumble or criticize us when we ask for wisdom. He knows that we are weak, and he is happy to answer our prayer for wisdom.

Yet sometimes we hesitate to ask because our own failures discourage us. At such times, we need to remember that our hope is not in ourselves but in God who will never give up on us. There is a Chinese saying, "The wise doubt not; the kind worry not; the brave fear not." A wise Christian should not doubt God's love even in times of crisis.

James then explains *how* one must ask God for wisdom: "When you ask, you must believe and not doubt, because the one who doubts is like a wave of the sea, blown and tossed by the wind" (1:6). When someone asks God for wisdom but refuses to act on it, or asks God for wisdom but doubts his

---

9. Dale C. Allison, *James: A Critical and Exegetical Commentary*, ICC (New York: Bloomsbury, 2013), 172.

goodness and doesn't believe he will provide it, he/she is unstable like a wave on the sea, tossed around by the winds, aimless and directionless.

James's words may have reminded his Jewish readers of a similar image in Isaiah: "The wicked are like the tossing sea, which cannot rest, whose waves cast up mire and mud" (Isa 57:20). If so, they might have grasped that he was implying that those who doubt God's provision of wisdom are very like "the wicked" – the group described in Psalm 1 as being "like chaff that the wind blows away" (Ps 1:4). Sophie Laws says, "The double-minded are the archetypal sinners; for James doubleness is of the essence of human sin, seen in the divisive desires of the individual (v.1) and the 'adulterous' attempts to combine prayer to God and a quest for the friendship of the world."[10]

The word that the NIV translates as "doubt" is translated in the KJV as "wavering" (1:6). "Doubt" or "wavering" does not focus on intellectual uncertainty (as if one doesn't comprehend an event) but on uncertain loyalty (as if one doesn't *believe* that God can help). Someone who is not fully committed to the Lord "should not expect to receive anything from the Lord" (1:7). Someone who does not trust God's goodness to give wisdom not only forfeits God's wisdom but also everything else God might give them. Remember King Solomon: When he asked God for wisdom, God responded by saying,

> Since you have asked for [wisdom] . . . I will give you a *wise* and *discerning heart* . . . Moreover, I will give you what you have not asked for – both *wealth* and *honor* – so that in your lifetime you will have *no equal among kings*. And if you walk in obedience to me and keep my decrees and commands as David your father did, I will give you *a long life*. (1 Kgs 3:11–14, italics added)

When someone seeks wisdom, God grants far more than what is asked. But those who doubt God's goodness to give wisdom, receive neither wisdom nor the other blessings associated with wisdom (such as endurance in times of trouble).

Sometimes we ask God for wisdom when we need to decide between two jobs, two colleges, two ministries, or two potential future spouses. When we do this, we need to be careful that our request is not mere lip service. We need to patiently wait for him to reveal his will. When we ask God for wisdom, we must wholeheartedly believe that he will grant it, and we must listen for his answer. When we do this, we make it clear that we trust God.

---

10. Sophie Laws, *The Epistle of James* (Peabody, MA: Hendrickson, 1980), 184.

Those who are overwhelmed by internal disputes are divided within themselves. The Chinese describe someone like this as trying to stand with their feet in two boats – an extremely precarious position that will inevitably result in a humiliating fall. Such a person cannot attain God's wisdom. James is thinking in similar terms when he describes a doubter as "double-minded and unstable in all they do" (1:8).[11] This description applies to someone like Lot's wife, who left Sodom but still looked back to it with longing.[12] Another Chinese saying, "Three hearts and two wills" similarly conveys the idea that failure to be single-minded leads to disastrous decisions. A divided mind and divided loyalties leave a person "unstable," like the wind-tossed wave James referred to in 1:6.

We get more insight into the meaning of the word "unstable" when we note that James uses it again in 3:8, where he writes: "No human being can tame the tongue. It is a restless [unstable] evil, full of deadly poison." Just as an uncontrolled tongue can shift between praising God and cursing people, so an uncontrolled mind can shift between trusting God and doubting his goodness. A person who is double-minded may simultaneously believe that God can give wisdom and be unwilling to wait upon God to receive wisdom. *Every* action of such a double-minded person ("all they do") is unstable. They always waver and can never reach the destination God intends for them. They are like people who say they want to learn how to swim but insist on keeping one foot on the ground.

James does not want his readers to be like that. He wants them to single-mindedly trust God for wisdom in their trials, humbly ask God for wisdom, wholeheartedly believe that he will give it, and gratefully receive it since God generously gives wisdom to anyone who sincerely asks for it.

Without God's provision of wisdom, it would be impossible for us to press on along the path to perfection or spiritual maturity. As we acknowledge our vulnerability and our need for God's help, we must trust God to grant us wisdom, and we must believe without wavering. God is willing to help us and is wholeheartedly committed to us. But if we become hesitant

---

11. The word "double-minded" could literally be translated as two-souled. James is the first to use the expression and may even have invented it. Stanley E. Porter, "Is *Dipsuchos* (James 1:8; 4:8) a 'Christian' Word?" *Biblica* 71, no. 4 (1990): 469–498. In the late first or mid-second century, the author of the *Shepherd of Hermas* interpreted "double-minded" as meaning not setting one's heart towards the Lord (Vision 3.10). For a detailed study of this word in the Septuagint, Dead Sea Scrolls, and the Apostolic Fathers, see Luke L. Cheung, *The Genre, Composition and Hermeneutics of James* (Carlisle: Paternoster, 2003), 197–200.
12. 1 Clement 23.1–2.

or double-minded and respond to him halfheartedly, we will fail to receive wisdom or other wisdom-related blessings from God.

1:9–11 Loving God with all your strength/possessions

James has addressed how true worshipers trust God with their *lives* ("your soul") in the midst of persecution and the importance of being *single-minded* ("loving God with all your heart") when asking for and receiving wisdom from God. Now he addresses the third instruction in the Shema: "Love God with all your strength."

"Strength" is a positive trait; someone who is in a *strong* position economically is someone who is rich or wealthy. People in James's day thought (as some still do) that the rich are favored by God. But James thought otherwise: "Believers in humble circumstances ought to take pride in their high position" (1:9). It is not our economic status, but our spiritual state, that determines our identity. In saying this, James is reflecting what the Lord Jesus said: "Blessed are the poor in spirit, for theirs is the kingdom of heaven; Blessed are the meek, for they will inherit the earth" (Matt 5:3, 5).[13] Our spiritual blessedness is not dependent on our economic status but on our status before God – if we are his children, both heaven and earth are ours.

In James's day, as in ours, the poor were often oppressed and exploited, while the rich acted with impunity, escaping judgment and punishment. As early as the mid-eighth century BC, prophets like Amos and Zephaniah spoke against such injustices. Amos, for example, accused his fellow Jews of taking the poor as debt-slaves (Amos 2:6; 8:6), making dishonest trades (Amos 8:5–6), and bribing judges (Amos 5:10, 12). The poor were humiliated while the rich lived extravagantly (Amos 2:7–8; 3:15; 5:11; 6:4–6; see also Isa 2:9–12; Zeph 3:11–13). James knows that his readers face similar injustices. But he does not want them to focus on their poverty; instead, he wants them to focus on their "high position" in God's sight – their salvation.

James does not use the term "poor" in 1:9. Instead, he speaks of those in "humble circumstances." What he says applies not only to those who are economically destitute but also to any of us who have a lower economic or social status than others with whom we interact. James is saying that we should not be humiliated by our humble circumstances – a useful reminder in a world

---

13. The theme of the rich becoming poor, and the poor becoming rich has a long history, ranging from Hannah's song (1 Sam 2:1–10) to Mary's *Magnificat* (Luke 1:46–55). For more on this theme of eschatological reversal, see Cheung, *Genre*, 252–260.

where materialism is spreading like wildfire and people use social media to boast of their possessions.

Later, James uses the same word, "humble," to refer to those who are humble before God and turn to God in true repentance (4:6–9). He tells his readers to "humble yourselves before the Lord, and he will lift you up" (4:10). Those who do this will be exalted, regardless of their economic or social status.

The word translated "take pride" (1:9) in the NIV can also be translated "boast" (see the ESV, NRSV). It means something like "have confidence." That is how Jeremiah used it:

"Let not the wise boast of their wisdom
or the strong boast of their strength
or the rich boast of their riches
but let the one who boasts boast about this:
that they have the understanding to know me,
that I am the LORD, who exercises kindness,
justice and righteousness on earth,
for in these I delight,"
declares the LORD. (Jer 9:23–24)

To sum up: We can be confident and rejoice in our spiritual status, regardless of our economic or social circumstances, since God's love and faithfulness are not affected by our poverty or our wealth.

We can now understand why the poor have a reason to rejoice and why James tells the rich that they can "take pride in their humiliation" (1:10a). When rich Jews accepted the Lord, the Jewish community ostracized them, and so they became poor and were humiliated.[14] But they were not to be ashamed of their faith in Christ because it is a pearl that is worth more than all their previous riches (see Matt 13:44–46).

James 1:10 also implies that the rich should take pride in their humility as much as in their humiliation. In other words, the rich should rejoice to acknowledge that they are human, like everyone else, and so are dependent on God for all they are and all they possess. Too often, those who are rich think that their wealth guarantees their future. But it does nothing of the kind, as

---

14. This view is argued by C. L. Mitton, *The Epistle of James* (London: Marshall, Morgan & Scott, 1966), 39, and Fenton J. A. Hort, *The Epistle of St. James* (London: Macmillan, 1909), 15.

we know from the many stories about people in Vietnam who buried gold to keep it safe and then could not find the place they had hidden it.[15]

Wealth can even destroy those who possess it[16] – a point driven home by the sad fate of Jack Whittaker, a man who won US $314 million in a jackpot in 2002. Within a few years his marriage broke down, his granddaughter died of a drug overdose, and the money was gone.[17]

James reminds his readers that, like wild flowers, "the rich will fade away even while they go about their business" (1:10b–11; Isa 40:6–8).[18] In the Judean and Arabian wilderness, wild flowers sometimes bloom in the morning while dew covers the grass. But by midday the dry wind and the scorching heat of the sun wither the flowers. In the same way, the wealthy may appear to have everything they want and be confident of a prosperous future, only to have it all evaporate. Jesus warned people that riches cannot be trusted when he told the parable of the rich person who died just when he assumed he was secure (Luke 12:13–21). The rich should realize the vanity of wealth and live humbly: they should only take pride in their humility.

Ultimately, our economic status has little bearing on our spirituality. So if we are poor, we should take pride in our high status in God; if we are rich, we should take pride in being humble before God. God allows us to be poor or wealthy – he alone makes that decision. Our focus should not be on our wealth or poverty. Like Agur son of Jakeh, we should pray: "I ask of you, LORD . . . give me neither poverty nor riches, but give me only my daily bread. Otherwise, I may have too much and disown you and say, 'Who is the LORD?' Or I may become poor and steal, and so dishonor the name of my God" (Prov 30:7–9).

Our ultimate trust should be in God. He is the one who gives us the wisdom we need to endure trials of any kind.

1:12 Blessing of perseverance

James concludes this section on loving God with one's soul, heart, and strength by returning to the themes of trials, testing, and perseverance. He repeats what he said in 1:2–4 in the form of beatitude, like those Jesus uttered in the Sermon on the Mount (Matt 5:3–11). James's beatitude reads: "Blessed is the

15. Allison J. Truitt, *Dreaming of Money in Ho Chi Minh City* (Seattle: University of Washington Press, 2013), 69–70.
16. Pedrito U. Maynard-Reid, *Poverty and Wealth in James* (Maryknoll: Orbis, 1987), 42–43.
17. http://www.wisebread.com/people-who-became-millionaires-overnight-and-what-they-did-with-the-money.
18. Other OT writers used similar images to illustrate the transience of human life (Job 14:2; Pss 90:6; 103:15–16).

one who perseveres under trial because, having stood the test, that person will receive the crown of life that the Lord has promised to those who love him" (1:12; see also 5:11).[19]

In the OT, blessing was associated with enjoying God's protection, which he promised to those who kept the covenant he made with his people at Sinai. In Jewish thinking, this meant that only the Jews enjoyed God's blessing. But James, like Jesus, looks beyond the Jewish nation. Anyone who trusts in God can enjoy his blessing, provided they continue to trust God in the midst of their trials.

Their reward will be "the crown of life" (1:12a). James's readers would have been familiar with the laurel wreaths given as crowns to the victors in athletic contests in the Greco-Roman world (1 Cor 9:25) and with the gem-studded crowns worn by royalty (see, for example, 2 Sam 12:30). James wants them to know that there is an even greater crown awaiting them, "the crown of life," a metaphor for the fullness of life. So, they were to face trials, persecution, and even death, confident in the knowledge that the fullness of life awaited them. John refers to a similar promise: "Do not be afraid of what you are about to suffer. I tell you, the devil will put some of you in prison to test you, and you will suffer persecution for ten days. Be faithful, even to the point of death, and I will give you life as your victor's crown" (Rev 2:10). These words are particularly encouraging for those who face martyrdom because of their faith in Christ.

James does, however, include a caveat: This "crown of life" is only for "those who love him" (1:12b). People can endure trials and persecution for many reasons. In Asia, for example, people have been known to set themselves on fire as a form of protest.[20] James makes it clear that the crown of life is not for anyone who endures any form of trial for any reason; it is specifically for those who love God and endure trials because of their love for him.

Christians, then and now, do not have the option of avoiding suffering. In fact, Paul warns Timothy that "everyone who wants to live a godly life in Christ Jesus will be persecuted" (2 Tim 3:12). So we should never think that our trials are a curse or punishment from God. They are sometimes permitted by God, who uses them to purify us. They could even be described as

---

19. The OT beatitudes had a set pattern: a statement of "blessedness," a noun or pronoun in the absolute form (always with reference to a person, never a thing or state), and a relative clause that defined the kind of person involved (e.g., "Blessed are all who take refuge in him" Ps 2:12; see also Ps 34:8; Dan 12:12). Sometimes, it had parallel lines of description, blessing, and promise (see Pss 1:1–2; 32:1–2; 41:2–4; 65:4; Prov 3:13; 8:34–36).
20. http://www.dailymail.co.uk/news/article-2566828/Indian-farmer-dies-dousing-petrol-setting-fire- protest-land- ownership.html.

blessings in disguise, for God can use them to refine us. That is why we are to rejoice during suffering by counting our blessings. So let us strive to suffer well, persevering in our faith, relying on the wisdom that God will supply, and knowing God is with us.

1:13–18 Distinguishing between Trials and Temptations

After explaining how to endure *trials* (1:2–12), James turns to the related question of how to face *temptations* (1:13–18). In Greek, these two words are homographs – words that have the same spelling but different meanings.[21] An English example is the word *tear*: it may refer to a tear in one's eyes or a tear (rip) in one's clothing. James uses these similar words but reminds his readers that while trials are to be endured, temptations are to be avoided. We should not blame God for the temptations we face (1:13). To put it another way, trials are neutral; what matters is how we respond to them. If we respond by sinning, then the trial becomes a temptation to sin. But it is not the trial itself that is sinful; rather, it is our own desires that leave us vulnerable to temptation (1:14–15). God who is good gives only good gifts, not temptations (1:16–18).

1:13 Temptations do not come from God

James has no problem with the statement that "Jesus was led by the Spirit into the wilderness" where he would face testing (Matt 4:1a), as Abraham and the Israelites in the desert had (Gen 22:1; Deut 8:2). But he doesn't believe temptations come from God. Instead, temptations come either from the evil one (as in Matthew 4:1b – "to be tempted by the devil") or from our own desires.

James insists, "When tempted, no one should say, 'God is tempting me.'" His reason for saying this is rooted in God's character: "God cannot be tempted by evil, nor does he tempt anyone" (1:13).[22] But doesn't the word "cannot" contradict God's omnipotence? How can we say that there is something that the all-powerful God cannot do? The answer to this question is quite simple. God cannot do things that are incompatible with his holy character. King David put it like this: "You are not a God who is pleased with wickedness; with you, evil people are not welcome" (Ps 5:4). Because God is holy, evil has no appeal to him – in fact, it appalls him. And he wants his people to be like him: "I am the LORD your God; consecrate yourselves and be holy, because

---

21. Isaacs writes, "In Greek the nouns *peirasmos* and its cognate verb *peirazein* can mean either [trials or temptation]," thus understanding them as homographs. Marie E. Isaacs, "Suffering in the Lives of Christians: James 1:2–19A," *Review & Expositor* 97, no. 2 (2000): 183–193.
22. James used an emphatic pronoun "himself" (*autos*) to indicate the absolute impossibility of God tempting anyone.

I am holy" (Lev 11:44). A holy God cannot be accused of encouraging his people to engage in sinful behavior. He does not tempt them and he helps them when they are tempted. Temptations come from sources other than God.

1:14–15 Temptations originate in our own desires

If God does not tempt people, where do temptations come from? In the case of both Job and Jesus, the devil was involved (Job 1:6–12; Matt 4:1). So does this mean that when Christians succumb to temptation, they can use the excuse, "the devil made me do it"?

James does not deny that the devil may play a role in shaping the form in which temptation comes, but he insists that to put all the blame for temptation on God or the devil is an evasion of personal responsibility: "Each person is tempted when they are dragged away by their own evil desire and enticed" (1:14).

James is not saying that desire itself is evil. The word "desire" is neutral, in both Greek and English. Jesus offers us an example of good desire when he says, "I have eagerly desired to eat this Passover with you before I suffer" (Luke 22:15). He also offers us an example of evil desire when he says, "You want to carry out your father's [Satan's] desires. He was a murderer from the beginning, not holding to the truth, for there is no truth in him" (John 8:44).[23]

The above examples also show that we cannot limit "desires" to sexual desires, as is often done.[24] Sexual desire, too, is neutral – sex is a gift God has given us and so sexual desire is not wrong. Like all other desires, it becomes wrong when we allow it to lead us into sin.

So what makes a desire bad? The clue lies in the two verbs James uses: "dragged away" and "enticed." The Greek translation of the OT used the same word to refer to Joseph's being "pulled . . . up" or "dragged up" (TLV) out of a pit and sold to Midianite traders (Gen 37:28). Joseph lost control of his life, and so does anyone who is overpowered and dragged away by desire. If this happens, God is no longer in control of that person's life.

No one should blame God for their own actions. For example, wanting to eat is a neutral desire. But the desire to eat becomes evil when it leads one

---

23. For a list of other evil desires, see Mark 4:19; Rom 1:24; 6:12; Gal 5:16, 24; 1 Pet 1:14; 2 Pet 2:10; 1 John 2:16–17. For the understanding of evil inclination in Jewish tradition, see Cheung, *Genre*, 206–213.
24. Wolmarans argues that this section refers only to sexual temptation (Johannes L. P. Wolmarans, "Misogyny as a Meme: The Legacy of James 1:12–18," *Acta Patristica et Byzantina* 17 [2006]: 349–361), McKnight disagrees. Scot McKnight, *The Letter of James*, NICNT (Grand Rapids: Eerdmans, 2011), 245.

to eat more than one's fair share of the food while others go hungry. This is one of the sins Paul rebuked when some in the church of Corinth allowed their greed to disrupt the Lord's Supper (1 Cor 11:17–22). By indulging their desires, the Corinthians were harming others. It has been said, "Even though you have ten thousand fields, you can eat but one measure of rice a day." Our legitimate desire for wealth and security can easily slip into the greed that makes us hoard possessions and reject all limits.

The other verb James uses is "enticed." Traps are baited with something that looks good. Fish or animals are drawn to the baits and become victims of the traps. The same is true when we are "enticed" by our desires. The book of Proverbs provides a good example of enticement when it talks about how an adulterous woman tries to attract a young man's attention:

> I came out to meet you; I looked for you and have found you! I have covered my bed with colored linens from Egypt. I have perfumed my bed with myrrh, aloes and cinnamon. Come, let's drink deeply of love till morning; let's enjoy ourselves with love! My husband is not at home; he has gone on a long journey. (Prov 7:15–19)

The Apostle Peter also uses the word "entice" when he speaks of false teachers luring people away from the truth by appealing to their greed and desire for pleasure (2 Pet 2:14, 18).

Possibly because sexuality is often associated with desire and enticement, James uses a pregnancy metaphor to explain how desire can drag people into sin. Just as sex leads to conception, and conception to the birth of a child, who then grows to be an adult and bears further children, so "after desire has conceived, it gives birth to sin; and sin, when it is full-grown, gives birth to death" (1:15). We see this progression in the story of Adam and Eve. They experienced a desire to taste the forbidden fruit (the desire was "conceived"), and they allowed this desire to grow until they were "dragged away" by it, overcome by it, and sinned (Gen 3:6–19). God did not encourage them to sin; Satan did not force them to sin; it was their own uncontrolled desires that led to sin and death.

Pastors sometimes say that an evil desire comes first as a passer-by, then as an occasional guest, then as a frequent guest, and finally, as master of the house. Our experience tells us that this is true. When desires are not controlled or curtailed early on, they gather momentum and become a habit.

James is giving the same message that Jesus gave when he identified our inner being as the source of sin: "It is from within, out of a person's heart, that evil thoughts come – sexual immorality, theft, murder, adultery, greed, malice, deceit, lewdness, envy, slander, arrogance and folly. All these evils come from inside and defile a person" (Mark 7:20–23). Jesus knows that in this life we will always face temptation. It was something even he had to endure in his humanity (Heb 2:18; 4:15). But just as Jesus controlled his own desires for food, wealth, and power (Matt 4:1–11), we should not allow our desires to take a hold of us. We should imitate Jesus's example.

James, steeped in his Jewish heritage, may be reflecting on the blessing and cursing pattern of the Mosaic covenant, in which one course of action leads to life and another to death (Lev 26:1–39; Deut 28; 30:15–20). Those who respond to trials with faith and endurance will grow to perfection or maturity and enjoy the blessing of life (1:4, 12), while those who follow their desires and succumb to temptation are on the path that leads to death (1:15).

| In trials | – Faith | → Patience | → Perfection/Crown of Life |
| In temptations | – Desire | → Sin | → Death |

As noted earlier, the words translated "trials" and "temptations" are homophones, showing how closely these two concepts are related. So, how do we handle trials while resisting temptation? As James has already said: "If any of you lacks wisdom, you should ask God, who gives generously to all without finding fault, and it will be given to you" (1:5). God wants us to succeed in our Christian lives and attain maturity or perfection. He will provide the wisdom we need. But God is willing to provide more than just wisdom; he is also the source of every good and perfect gift.

1:16–18 Good and perfect gifts come from God

James again addresses those he is writing to as "dear brothers and sisters" (see also 1:19; 2:5). He has a deep love for them. So, he does not want them to be deceived about who God is and what God does (1:16).[25]

God is not the source of temptations; but he is the source of "every good and perfect gift" (1:17a), including the good gift of wisdom. The wisdom that "comes from heaven is first of all pure; then peace-loving, considerate,

---

25. In the NT "deception" is often associated with moral failure (Matt 18:12–13; 1 Cor 6:9; 1 John 1:8).

submissive, full of mercy and *good* fruit, impartial and sincere" (3:17). God is the author of this wisdom and everything that comes with it.

God is also the source of every perfect gift. The word translated "perfect" comes from the word *telos*, which means purpose or goal. His perfect gifts are the gifts that lead us to maturity, wholeness, or completeness. Obviously, such gifts overlap with the gift of wisdom, but their focus is slightly different. We ask God for wisdom to handle particular situations, but he also gives us other gifts that lead us along the path to maturity.

James speaks of these good and perfect gifts as originating "from above," that is, from the heavenly dwelling of God (see 3:13). This, too, is a reminder that they originate with God.

James uses a unique title to describe the one who gives the gifts: "the Father of the heavenly lights, who does not change like shifting shadows" (1:17b). In Genesis, God is revealed as the creator of the heavenly lights: the sun, moon and stars (Gen 1:14–18; see also Ps 136:7; Jer 31:35). By linking the gifts to the creator of these lights, James is emphasizing that the good and perfect gifts share the goodness of God's whole creation. Whereas the heavenly lights change – the sun rises and sets, the moon waxes and wanes, the constellations change with the seasons – God, their creator, does not change. His radiance does not alter "like shifting shadows" (1:17). How could God's light change, for there is nothing dark about him! He has no tinge of evil (which is why he cannot be the source of temptation). God is pure light and the author of untarnished gifts that are as pure as he is. He is unchanging in his desire to bless humanity.

God's goodness is evident in the fact that he "chose to give us birth through the word of truth" (1:18a). God's word called the world into being (Gen 1), and God's work of redemption brought salvation through the message of the gospel (which James refers to as the "word of truth").[26] Paul used a similar phrase to refer to the gospel he preached (2 Tim 2:15), and the psalmist uses similar wording to refer to God's law (Ps 119:43). God demonstrates his unchanging faithfulness by giving James's audience new birth through what they have heard, "the word of truth" (meaning both the Scriptures and the gospel). Whereas temptations bring sin and death, God gives new life.[27]

God exalts those who have received the new birth as "firstfruits" of all that he created (1:18b). In the OT, firstfruits was the first yield of a harvest,

---

26. For a debate on this, see Allison, *James*, 281–285.
27. Note that both 1:15 and 1:18 use the pregnancy metaphor of giving birth.

which was consecrated and offered to God (Exod 22:29; Deut 18:4; Num 18:8–12). Just as the firstfruits were the prelude to the full harvest, so the renewed messianic people of God are the prelude to the new creation of the whole universe, the representative beginning of the redemption of all creation (Rom 8:21; 2 Cor 5:17; Gal 6:15; Eph 4:24).

What is striking here is that James reverses the OT practice: rather than people bringing the firstfruits to God, God himself appoints his people to be "a kind of firstfruits of all he created."[28] God has redeemed them and has given them new life, and now they are consecrated to him. What a wonderful gift! And how different from the unfounded accusation that God was giving them temptations!

The Japanese traditionally offered worship to the Seven Gods of Fortune, *shichi fukujin*, hoping to receive fortune, good luck, and prosperity in their business dealings. But the God to whom James directs our attention gives far more than that! He is the author of all wisdom, and every good and perfect gift and he is prepared to give generously if asked. So we should not hold back, but should ask God to give us his good gifts and his perfect gifts, and especially his gifts of salvation, redemption, and new life. And we should thank him for all he gives us since whatever we have – spiritual or material – comes from God.

We also need to remember that God's good gifts may include allowing trials that shape us into the people he wants us to be. These trials are intended for our good, and we should endure them. But when, during such trials, we are tempted by evil, we should not blame God for that temptation; instead, we should seek his help. Temptation arises from our desires. God doesn't tempt us; instead, he will provide us with an escape in the midst of trials if we only ask him (1 Cor 10:13).

1:19–27 PERFECT OBEDIENCE TO GOD'S LAW

Up to this point, James has structured his teaching around the principles of loving God in the way prescribed in the Shema. But it is not enough to love God and ignore everything else. Jewish teachers were well aware that the Shema involved practical obedience. So was the Lord Jesus, who explicitly linked the Shema with the command to "love your neighbor as yourself" and stressed that "all the Law and the Prophets hang on these two commandments" (Matt

---

28. Paul, too, referred to redeemed people in terms of *firstfruits*: Epaenetus was the firstfruit from Asia Minor [Turkey] (Rom 16:5), and Stephanus was the firstfruit of the province of Corinth in Achaia (1 Cor 16:15).

22:39–40). His reference to the Law and the Prophets is a reminder that the Christian life includes obedience to all that God has revealed in his word. There should be nothing surprising about this, for every country and kingdom insists that its citizens, residents, and visitors obey its laws, as President Xi Jinping of China said when speaking in America in 2017.[29] In the same way, those who are part of the kingdom of God need to live in obedience to the laws of that kingdom.

1:19–20 Living Wisely

Once again, James begins a new section of the letter by referring to his readers as his "dear brothers and sisters," and exhorting them to pay attention to what he is about to say. This pattern recurs throughout the letter. It is possible that the words "take note of this" are part of a formula that went with the type of proverbial advice James gives here, just as we might introduce some advice by saying, "Remember the old saying . . ."

We are still in James's prologue to his letter. The rest of the letter is an expansion of the saying, "everyone should be quick to listen, slow to speak and slow to become angry" (1:19):

Quick to listen	→ 1:21–25	→ 2:1–26	Listening results in action
Slow to speak	→ 1:26	→ 3:1–12	Speech must be weighed
Slow to anger	→ 1:20	→ 4:1–10	Love extinguishes anger

The instruction to be "quick to listen" echoes a recurrent theme in the book of Proverbs: "Let the wise *listen* and add to their learning, and let the discerning get guidance," and "*Listen*, my son [and daughter], to your father's instruction and do not forsake your mother's teaching" (Prov 1:5, 8; italics added).

Those who are quick to speak may not allow themselves adequate time to reflect on what they are about to say. This can be dangerous, for as James reminds us in a later passage, words can be like sparks that start uncontrollable fires (3:6). So he advises his readers to be "slow to speak."

Finally, James instructs them to be "slow to become angry" (1:19). This command fits well with being slow to speak, for when we are angry, hasty words spring to our lips. Douglas Moo puts it this way: "Uncontrolled anger leads to uncontrolled speech."[30] Such anger often results from failure to listen carefully to someone with whom we disagree.

---

29. http://www.scmp.com/news/china/diplomacy-defence/article/1860724/foreign-ngos-china-have-obey-chinese-law-president-xi.
30. Moo, *The Letter of James*, 82.

James's instructions to his Jewish readers in the first century are equally applicable to us in Asia in the twenty-first century. We must be willing to listen carefully, to speak cautiously, and to respond calmly rather than react angrily. The Chinese have a saying, "If you are patient in one moment of anger, you will escape a hundred days of sorrow." James would agree. Anger has unfortunate consequences and "does not produce the righteousness that God desires" (1:20). Yet we often tend to act as if anger would make the world a better place. This starts in childhood when we throw tantrums when we think someone is not being fair to us, but it can carry on into adulthood when people riot or engage in violent protests against injustice. Anger and violence may sometimes bring justice but this is rare. In any event, angry outbursts are not the path to moral righteousness. Rather, we should respond to injustice with patient perseverance, as James has already reminded his readers (1:3–4).

James is not saying that anger is always wrong. He says that we should be "slow to become angry," not that we should never be angry. The Lord Jesus himself became angry when he saw how traders were abusing God's temple and turning this house of prayer into a den of robbers (Matt 21:13). But his anger did not bubble up in an instant. He had visited the temple many times before he decided it was time to act against this abuse. Moreover, his anger was not roused by some personal slight; Jesus was driven by zeal for his Father's house (John 2:17).

1:21–25 Committing to Obey God's Law

James's greatest concern is believers' hearts, not merely their outward actions. So he advises his hearers to look within and "get rid of all moral filth and the evil that is so prevalent" (1:21a).[31] The word translated "get rid of" refers to someone taking off their outer clothing. The NT uses this metaphor to describe putting aside vices or sin (Rom 13:12; Eph 4:22, 25; Col 3:8; Heb 12:1; 1 Pet 2:1). In Zechariah 3, "getting rid of" is linked with "filth," as it is here in James. In that chapter, the prophet Zechariah describes a vision in which he sees God graciously sending an angel to exchange the high priest's "filthy clothes," which represent his sin, for the clean robes of a faithful priest. James wants his readers to experience a similar transformation.

The biblical writers not only speak of "putting off" something, but also ask their readers to "put on" something. Paul, for example, asks his readers to "put off" sin and "put on" righteousness. James, too, tells his readers to "get

---

31. The verse begins with "therefore" indicating this is a concluding statement.

rid of" evil and to "humbly accept the word planted in you, which can save you" (1:21b). This acceptance goes beyond simply accepting Christ into our lives. It refers to ongoing learning and understanding of God's word and its significance for us.

In speaking of the word having been "planted" in their hearts, James is referring to the fulfillment of the prophecies of Jeremiah and Ezekiel, both of whom looked forward to a time when God's new covenant would be established and God's word would be written on the hearts of God's people: "'This is the covenant I will make with the people of Israel after that time,' declares the LORD. 'I will put my law in their minds and write it on their hearts'" (Jer 31:33; see also Ezek 36:26–27).[32] That time has come, and the word of God has been implanted in the believers' hearts.[33] This implanted word is more powerful than any inborn wickedness like moral filth and evil.

The humility of accepting the implanted word contrasts with the sinful anger mentioned in 1:20.[34] Those in whom God has planted his word will be able to hear it, provided they are slow to speak and quarrel but quick to listen. When Christians listen to others (instead of always speaking or getting angry), they can also hear what God is saying through his word, which "can save you." This salvation involves both deliverance from a physical harm that can follow a heated argument and deliverance from God's future judgment (see also 4:12; 5:9b).

Being a good listener to God's word is not enough; one must also act on what is heard. The OT clearly taught, "You must *obey* my laws and be careful to follow my decrees. I am the LORD your God. *Keep* my decrees and laws, for the man who *obeys* them will live by them. I am the LORD" (Lev 18:4–5; italics added). James knew his Jewish readers would have listened to the reading of this law each week when they worshiped in the synagogues, and so he writes, "Do not merely listen to the word, and so deceive yourselves. Do what it says" (1:22).[35] When believers read God's word, they should be seeking not just information but transformation.

---

32. See James H. Ropes, *Epistle of St. James*, ICC (Edinburgh: T & T Clark, 1916), 173, and James B. Adamson, *The Epistle of James*, NICNT (Grand Rapids: Eerdmans, 1976), 34, 81.

33. This doesn't mean that the entire Bible is in one's heart; instead, the basic principles of the *Torah*, the law, are in a believer's heart. The best way to saturate oneself with God's word is to keep studying the Bible. The more we study it, the more our hearts will be saturated with his word.

34. The rabbis of James's era taught that meekness or humbleness gave a person credibility in interpreting the Law of Moses – see George F. Moore, *Judaism* (Peabody: Hendrickson, 1997), 2:245. James, too, purposefully combines humility and God's word in 1:21.

35. Paul gives much the same teaching in Romans 2:13.

James gives a vivid illustration of the foolishness of the type of listening that involves nothing more than "in one ear and out the other": "Anyone who listens to the word but does not do what it says is like someone who looks at his face in a mirror and, after looking at himself, goes away and immediately forgets what he looks like" (1:23–24).[36] The reason we look at ourselves in a mirror is to make sure that our faces are clean and our hair combed. It would be foolish to look in a mirror, see that one's face is dirty and one's hair disheveled, and then immediately forget about it, so that one neither washes one's face nor combs one's hair.[37] Why bother to look in the mirror at all if we are not going to act on what we see there? The same question could be asked of anyone who listens to God's word but doesn't change their life on the basis of God's instructions. What is the point of looking into the word to learn the truth of God and the reality about ourselves but refusing to acknowledge and act on what we see?

Those who actively respond to what they see in the mirror of God's word are blessed: "But whoever looks intently into the perfect law . . . and continues in it – not forgetting what they have heard, but doing it – they will be blessed in what they do" (1:25). In saying this, James is echoing Jesus's words, "Blessed . . . are those who hear the word of God and obey it" (Luke 11:28). Their lives stand firmly on the rock of God's word (Matt 7:24–27).

Had James lived in China, he might have used "magic mirrors" as his example. These polished bronze mirrors are similar to ancient Roman and Greek mirrors, except that in bright sunshine the light seems to penetrate the mirror and make designs on the back of the mirror. These designs can be projected onto a dark wall or surface.[38] Similarly, the light of the word of God penetrates people's hearts and reveals their innermost thoughts. But if, after seeing the pattern of their hearts, believers make no attempt to change their lifestyle, there is no point in looking into the word of God. We are to be more than mere hearers of the word of God; we are to be doers of God's word.

The "mirror" James is referring to is "the perfect [*telos*] law." He previously used the word *telos* in regard to the *maturity* (perfection) that comes with

---

36. For a study of similarities between these verses and Plato's *Alcibiades*, see Nicholas Denyer, "Mirrors in James 1:22–25 and Plato, *Alcibiades*, 132c–133c," *Tyndale Bulletin* 50, no. 2 (1999): 237–240.

37. The word translated *forget* in James 1:24 was used frequently in the Septuagint translation of the OT in exhorting the people of Israel not to forget God, his covenants, and his commandments (Deut 4:23; 6:2; 26:13). Thus, James makes yet another connection to the teachings of the OT.

38. Robert K. G. Temple, "Magic Mirrors," *The Courier*, October 1988, 16.

perseverance (1:4) and the *perfect* gifts that come from God (1:17). James is saying that God's word, the law, is perfect and by it those who keep the law attain perfection.[39]

James also says that this perfect law "gives freedom." The Jews thought of freedom in terms of deliverance from slavery, as when God freed them from Egypt and made them his people who would serve him alone. So when James speaks of "the perfect law that gives freedom," he is thinking of the implanted word of God that frees those who love Christ from the burden of sin and guilt and sets them free to love God and their neighbors. This explains the paradox of "law" (which seems to imply constraints) and "freedom." Obedience to God's law brings inner freedom from the tyranny of self-indulgence and self-deception, and gives us freedom to choose to do the will of God.[40]

1:26–27 Examples of Loving Obedience

The adjective *religious* and the noun *religion* are rarely used in the NT. Some Christians think that these words have negative connotations of mysticism, asceticism, or ultraconservatism. But in the NT, they are used with both positive (Acts 26:5) and negative (Col 2:18) meanings. James uses these words in a positive sense, as marks of a true religion, and gives three examples of *how* believers can demonstrate their obedience to God's word by controlling their tongues (1:26), caring for widows, refugees, and orphans (1:27a), and not polluting themselves by accepting the world's standards and philosophies (1:27b). In these verses James is again introducing topics that he will expand on later in the letter.[41]

Controlling one's tongue	→ 1:26	→ 3:1–12; 4:11–17
Caring for the poor	→ 1:27a	→ 2:2–16; 5:1–6; 2:1–26
Avoiding worldliness	→ 1:27b	→ 3:13–4:10

---

39. *Telos* implies a purpose. The purpose of the law is to make those who read and obey it become mature. For various options on the meaning of the "perfect law," see Peter H. Davids, *James*, NIGTC (Grand Rapids: Eerdmans, 1982), 99–100.

40. Wall suggests that the "law that gives freedom" refers to the law of Jubilee (Leviticus 25), so that "freedom" referred to is the liberty granted to the poor and the oppressed. Robert W. Wall, *Community of the Wise: The Letter of James*, NTC (Valley Forge: Trinity Press International, 1997), 93–95.

41. James's placement of these topics forms a *chiasm* or ABBA pattern, where the first and last sections speak of the same topic and the middle two sections speak of another, common topic.

1:26 Controlling one's tongue

Just as some people deceive themselves by thinking they are religious merely because they read or listen to the word of God, even though they do not obey it (1:23–25), so others deceive themselves by not controlling their tongues. James has no patience with this. He writes: "Those who consider themselves religious and yet do not keep a tight rein on their tongues deceive themselves, and their religion is worthless" (1:26).

Reins attached to a bit are used by riders to control or direct an animal, a point that James returns to in chapter 3: "When we put bits into the mouths of horses to make them obey us, we can turn the whole animal" (3:3).[42] When a horse is kept on a tight rein, it is under control and not free to wander as it chooses. Similarly, those who obey God must keep their tongues under control and be "slow to speak and slow to become angry" (1:19). They should never be open to accusations that they lie, flatter, or slander others.

Today, some Christians tolerate sins of the tongue (or of the thumb in the case of social media). They treat gossip and insults as a trivial matter. But James is adamant that the religion of those who fail to control their tongues is "worthless" (1:26). This same word is used to refer to worshiping a false god (Acts 14:15; Rom 1:21; Eph 4:17). When those who say that they worship the true God, YHWH, utter harmful or hurtful words against their neighbors, they are behaving just like people who worship false gods or idols. True religion demands that we control our speech.

1:27a Caring for widows and orphans

After pointing out a way to identify false religiosity, James explains true religiosity: "Religion that God our Father accepts as pure and faultless is this: to look after orphans and widows in their distress" (1:27a). In the ancient world, widows and orphans were often helpless and impoverished. They had to rely on the charity of others to meet their basic physical needs for food and clothing.

James's statement is solidly rooted in the OT: "Do not take advantage of the widow or the fatherless [orphans]" (Exod 22:22; see also Lev 19:9–10, 33; Deut 10:17–19; Prov 19:17; 21:3; 31:9; Isa 3:5, 14–15; Amos 2:6–8; Zech 7:8–10; see also Matt 6:1–4). God commanded that such people be cared for because that is part of his character: "A father to the fatherless, a defender of widows, is God in his holy dwelling" (Ps 68:5). James wants those who believe

---

42. This metaphor of a bridle as an instrument for controlling one's evil desires is also used in the non-canonical writing the *Shepherd of Hermas* (Mandate 12.1–2).

in God to be like him and share his concerns – that is what makes for "pure and faultless" religion or piety.

In today's world, the homeless, migrants, and refugees often find themselves in a similar position to widows and orphans in ancient times. As Christians, we should care for them, both collectively (as churches) and individually. In doing so we reflect the true nature of our religion and show that our hearts resemble the heart of our Father.

1:27b Refusing to accept the world's values

The values and philosophies of the societies in which we live are often very different from the values set out in God's word. In fact, they often contradict them. James is referring to this when he says, "Religion that God our Father accepts as pure and faultless is this . . . to keep oneself from being polluted by the world" (1:27b). God's word, when properly implanted, is capable of building a powerful firewall, a robust immune system that can help believers detect and destroy the deadly viruses from this ungodly world that would pollute their value system.

JAMES 2:1-26

MATURITY, FAITH, AND OBEDIENCE

James is first and foremost a pastor. As such, his concern isn't so much that people know the law, but that they live by it, like those who look at mirrors and then make some changes (1:25). He has already reminded his readers of the importance of loving God (1:2–18) and emphasized that perfect obedience to God's law includes loving their neighbors (1:19–27). Now, in chapter 2, he illustrates how faith fulfills the law.[1]

He begins by pointing out that God abhors favoritism, and so those with true faith will not give preference to the rich (2:1–7). Faith will also provide for the basic needs of the poor, instead of sending them away with easy platitudes (2:15–16).

True faith is the *living* faith that Abraham and Rahab demonstrated by risking what was infinitely precious to them – Abraham, his son's life (2:21–24), and Rahab, her own life (2:25). Just as the human body without the spirit, is dead, so faith without obedient actions is dead (2:26).

Since the Reformation with its strong emphasis on *sola fide* ("by faith alone"), Christians have sometimes been reluctant to speak of faith and works in the same sentence. But James boldly asserts that genuine faith must lead to demonstrable works. Have we Asian Christians grasped this connection? Do our cultural and social practices contradict our faith?

Some Indian Christians accept the cultural notion of castes and will only choose spouses for their children from the same caste as theirs. But a living faith will not view people in terms of their caste. In most Asian countries, many people lack food, shelter, and clothing. Do we Christians care for their spiritual needs while ignoring their physical needs? When we do this, we seem phony to them and we fail to be like Jesus, who not only taught the five thousand but also cared about their hunger and tiredness and fed them with bread and fish.

2:1-13 FAITH AND FAVORITISM

Once again, James begins a new section of his letter by affectionately addressing his readers as "My brothers and sisters," but this time he also reminds them

---

1. James uses "faith" thirteen times between 2:1–26, illustrating that faith is his theme in this section.

that they are "believers in our glorious Lord Jesus Christ" (2:1). The adjective "glorious" was traditionally associated with God (Pss 24:7–10; 29:3; Num 24:11),[2] and by using it James is reminding his readers that the one in whom they believe has the same status as YHWH in the OT.

He then issues a stern command not to show favoritism or partiality (2:1).[3] Whether the context was religious – where the rich were given preferential places in worship (see 1 Cor 11:20–22) or legal – where the rich received favorable judgment[4] – James's command was the same: "Do not show favoritism." A living faith has no place for partiality or favoritism.

2:1 Do Not Show Favoritism

In honor-shame cultures like those in Asia, one must avoid embarrassment or humiliation at all cost. Humiliation is referred to as "losing face," and honor as "giving someone face," that is, making someone look good before others. The word translated "favoritism" in James has a similar meaning and implies showing special favor to some and not to others. James, basing his teaching on the OT command: "Do not pervert justice; do not show partiality to the poor or favoritism to the great, but judge your neighbor fairly" (Lev 19:15), explicitly warns Christians against the sin of favoritism or partiality.

Favoritism within a family is common in the Bible. Jacob, for example, gave his eleventh son, Joseph, preferential treatment. "When his brothers saw that their father loved him more than any of them, they hated him and could not speak a kind word to him" (Gen 37:4). Their hatred led them to capture him and secretly sell him as a slave, bringing great grief to their father.

Favoritism or partiality may not always be obvious to those practicing it, but is obvious to the victims. When a car driven by a rich Bollywood actor ran over and killed a homeless man on a pavement in Mumbai, no one was surprised that the actor was not charged for his crime for more than thirteen

---

2. See also Macc 2:8; 1 Enoch 25:7; 36:4; 40:3; 63:2.
3. Felder regards James 2:1–13 as a single pericope in which James stresses the theme of partiality three times: in 2:1 with *prosôpolêmpsia* ("partiality"), in 2:9 with *prosôpolêmteô* ("show partiality), and in 2:4 with *diakrinô* ("discriminate"). Cain Hope Felder, "Partiality and God's Law: An Exegesis of James 2:1–13," *The Journal of Religious Thought* 39, no. 2 (1982): 51–69. In addition, James uses a Greek construction (negative prohibition plus the vocative) to indicate that he is beginning a new section (2:1; see also 3:1; 4:11; 5:12).
4. Roy Bowen Ward, for example, argues that the context in James is legal proceedings rather than a gathering for worship. "Partiality in the Assembly: James 2:2–4," *Harvard Theological Review* 62, no. 1 (1969): 87–97. See also, Alicia Batten, "God in the Letter of James: Patron or Benefactor?" *NTS* 50 (2004): 257–272.

years. He was rich and the victim was poor.[5] Similarly, people often tend not to notice the slights endured by the poor, homeless, women, or children. But we who believe in "our glorious Lord Jesus Christ" have no excuse for not seeing people the way God sees them and for not acting in their defense. There is no excuse for being partial or showing favoritism.

2:2–4 Favoritism in the Church

Since the early days of the church, believers met to pray, fellowship, break bread, and listen to the apostles' teachings (Acts 2:42). At first, they met in the temple, then they met in local synagogues (Acts 9:20; 13:5; 14:1), and finally, in people's homes (Rom 16:5, 10, 15). James, who is writing to Jews of the middle era, places his example in the context of a synagogue (the Greek word translated as "your meeting" in 2.2 is actually *sunagoge*).

Synagogues were places for worship and also community centers where Jews met for fellowship, social gatherings, and political meetings.[6] In addition, they were the places where legal disputes within the community were heard and judgments given. So, James may be referring to favoritism in either a worship or a court setting.

Regardless of the setting, James's point about favoritism remains the same. He describes two men arriving at the synagogue. One is obviously wealthy, for he wears expensive clothes and gold jewelry. The other is poor – he has stained and shabby clothes. The judges offer the rich man a good seat along with them and tell the poor man to either stand or sit on the floor (2:2–3). Archaeological evidence of synagogues from the second century AD suggests that the rich would have been invited to sit on stools and the poor on mats spread out on the floor.[7] James denounces such behavior and asks, "Have you not discriminated among yourselves and become judges with evil thoughts?" Their actions show their partiality: they favor the rich. As such, they have become "judges with evil thoughts." They are no longer judging impartially. Favoritism has clouded their judgment. If they had a working faith, they would have treated both men equally and might even have offered their own chair to the poor man!

---

5. "Opinion," *The National*, Friday, January 13, 2017 (online version: https://www.thenation-al.ae/opinion/ comment/salman-khan-case-exposes-the-state-of-injustice-in-india-1.129313).
6. *TDNT*, 7.821–828.
7. R. Riesner, "Synagogues in Jerusalem," in *The Book of Acts in Its Palestinian Setting*, ed. Richard J. Bauckham (Grand Rapids: Eerdmans, 1995), 207–208.

James does not simply say such behavior is inappropriate. He says that those who act like this have "evil thoughts." He is putting partiality (discrimination or favoritism) in the same category as the evil thoughts Jesus referred to when he said that "it is from within, out of a person's heart, that evil thoughts come – sexual immorality, theft, murder, adultery, greed, malice, deceit, lewdness, envy, slander, arrogance and folly" (Mark 7:21–22). James's and Jesus's warnings should come as a shock to those of us who casually ignore partiality or practice discrimination.

James's reference to "judges" here recalls Leviticus 19:15: "Do not pervert justice; do not show partiality to the poor or favoritism to the great, but judge your neighbor fairly." God does not approve of discrimination based on outward appearances. Since he does not, neither should we who believe in our glorious Lord Jesus Christ.

2:5–11 Three Reasons for Avoiding Favoritism

James now gives three reasons for welcoming the poor rather than treating them with contempt. The first is theological: God has chosen the poor. The second is common sense: why give a special welcome to the rich, when they are the people who exploit you? And the third, which trumps all others, is that God's law requires it.

2:5 God's choice of the poor

The OT prophets often used the exhortation, "listen," to challenge people to pay serious attention to what they had to say (Isa 1:10; 28:14; Jer 2:4; Amos 3:1; 4:1; 5:1). In the same way, James starts with "listen," expresses his affection for his "dear brothers and sisters," and then challenges them: "Has not God chosen those who are poor in the eyes of the world to be rich in faith and to inherit the kingdom he promised those who love him?" (2:5). James is referring to Jesus's words in Luke 6:20: "Blessed are you who are poor, for yours is the kingdom of God" (see also Matt 5:3; 1 Cor 1:27–28). Jesus also said that it is "hard for someone who is rich to enter the kingdom of heaven" (Matt 19:23).

Poverty does not disqualify someone from entering God's kingdom. If the poor seek the Lord, he promises them entry into his kingdom. After all, the Israelites were impoverished slaves in Egypt when they cried out to God, and he delivered them. It is richness in faith, not material wealth that secures admittance into God's family.

The world neglects the poor and treats them as disposable. But God has chosen to honor and treasure them. Since our Father cares for the poor and rescues them, we his children should do the same. If we follow the world's pattern and show partiality to the rich, we are adopting the world's philosophies and values, which are incompatible with true religion (1:27).

We see one example of what it means to truly care for the poor in the work of Amy Carmichael in India. She noticed that Christians provided for the poor's basic needs but didn't give them what they themselves enjoyed – beauty and celebrations. So she set out to change that in *Dohnavur,* the orphanage that she built for them. Jeyaraj writes, "Carmichael and her coworkers also were careful to incorporate other Indian elements in the lives of the children. Hence, the architectural beauty of the buildings in *Dohnavur* blended into Indian landscape. For example, the House of Prayer is based on the model of an old palace in Travencore [a state in former India]."[8] She gave the children birthday parties, feasts when they entered adulthood (as is often done in India), grew gardens, and let the children decorate their rooms with flowers. Amy Carmichael offered God's kingdom of beauty for the poor. She understood that God had chosen the poor and that they should thus be treated with respect and offered the best we have.

2:6–7 Common sense theology

James's second reason for challenging his reader's partiality toward the rich is rooted in common sense. It is illogical for them to honor the rich and despise the poor when it is the rich who are doing them harm: "Is it not the rich who are exploiting you? Are they not the ones who are dragging you into court? Are they not the ones who are blaspheming the noble name of him to whom you belong?" (2:6–7). James is puzzled about why his listeners were honoring people who despised them (i.e., the rich), and despising those who honored them (i.e., the poor). Their behavior was illogical!

James's accusations against the rich are explicit. First, they were exploiting the Christians. Possibly, the rich were withholding their wages: "The wages you failed to pay the workers who mowed your fields are crying out against you. The cries of the harvesters have reached the ears of the Lord Almighty" (5:4). If the rich people were Jewish, as may well have been the case if they attended the synagogue, they knew that they were sinning by ignoring the words of the prophets and oppressing the poor (see Jer 7:6; 22:3; Ezek 18:12; 22:7, 29; Amos 4:1; 8:4; Zach 7:10; Mal 3:5). By favoring the rich (and oppressing the poor), the Christians were acting as if they approved of their actions. They were indeed acting like corrupt "judges with evil thoughts" (2:4).

---

8. Daniel Jeyaraj, "Amy Carmichael: The Child-Rescuing 'Amma,'" *American Baptist Quarterly* 24 (2005), 229.

Second, the rich were dragging poor believers into the law courts by instituting legal proceedings, possibly for repayment of debts or rents. These proceedings may have been similar to those the Lord Jesus referred to when he accused rich and influential Pharisees of devouring widow's houses, that is, using legal proceedings to evict widows from houses their husbands had owned (Mark 12:40). The poor are generally at a disadvantage in legal disputes. As an Asian Development Bank report says, "In India . . . the poorest members of society and firms unaffiliated with large business groups are most likely to be adversely affected by inaccessible, corrupt, or inefficient courts. The poor who find themselves defendants in criminal cases often do not have the resources to obtain bail. Moreover, when the defendant is the family breadwinner and cannot pay bail, his or her family loses its source of income."[9] That would have been the case even in James's time – the poor would have lost in the legal disputes. So it is shocking, and illogical, for Christians to favor the rich who use the court system to their own advantage and ignore the desperate plight of their victims.

Third, the rich were "blaspheming the noble name of him to whom you belong" (2:7). Here the verb "blaspheme" means "to speak in a disrespectful way that demeans, denigrates, maligns."[10] And the name that the rich were demeaning, denigrating, or maligning was the name of the one to whom the believers belong, the Lord Jesus Christ (1:1; 2:1; 5:10, 14; see also 1 Pet 4:14).[11] It is likely that they were denigrating his name by implying the poor were in trouble because they were Christians or by spreading rumors about the integrity of Christ and those who follow him.

James is not saying that being rich or enjoying a high status is wrong. God blessed people like Abraham, Job, David, and Solomon with wealth. Wealth is a blessing if gained honestly and used well and wisely as God intended. Wealth should never be used to exploit or oppress others, or to slander Christ or Christians.

2:8–11 Obedience to the law

James has already reminded his readers that they will "inherit the kingdom [God] promised to those who love him" (2:5). Like all kingdoms, God's

---

9. Asian Development Bank, *Challenges in Implementing Access to Justice Reform* (2005). A decade later, the situation remains the same.
10. BDAG, βλασφημέω (*blasphēmeō*).
11. James 2:7 forms an *inclusio* with James 2:1, emphasizing that the rich blasphemed the same good and glorious name of the Lord Jesus Christ that the believers adored.

kingdom has rules and regulations, including the royal (kingly) law, "Love your neighbor as yourself" (2:8b).[12] So James exhorts his readers, "If you really keep the royal law found in Scripture, 'Love your neighbor as yourself,' you are doing right" (2:8).

In the context of partiality, James is saying that those who treat all others equally "are doing right" (2:8), while those who show favoritism "sin and are convicted by the law as lawbreakers" (2:9). James presents this not as a hypothetical situation but as a real one.[13] Some in the congregation were guilty of showing favoritism and were thus sinning.[14]

Earlier, James explained the sequence of events that lead to sin: "Each person is tempted when they are dragged away by their own evil desire and enticed. Then, after desire has conceived, it gives birth to sin; and sin, when it is full-grown, gives birth to death" (1:14–15). That same pattern recurs here: the desire to avoid offending the rich gives birth to the sin of favoritism or partiality, and the law convicts those who commit this sin as "lawbreakers."

James's audience, who were mainly Jewish Christians who revered the Torah and considered themselves law-abiding, would have been horrified to be called "lawbreakers." They did not consider favoritism a "serious" sin. So, James spells it out for them: "Whoever keeps the whole law and yet stumbles at just one point is guilty of breaking all of it" (2:10). There are no percentage scores when it comes to keeping God's law. You don't get a "Pass" if you keep "enough" of it – 50% if you don't murder but do commit adultery; 80% if you don't murder or commit adultery but do show favoritism. There is only one verdict when it comes to keeping the law – Pass or Fail. Note that this does not mean all sins are equally serious. But James's point is that one cannot ignore partiality as a "minor" or "small" sin; it makes a person a lawbreaker just as any "major" sin like murder or adultery. Those who commit murder and adultery have clearly broken God's law, but so have those who show favoritism. All of them fall within the category of those who fail to keep God's royal law. They are all lawbreakers.[15]

James's use of parallelism drives his point home:

---

12. By calling the law the *royal* law (*basilikos*), James connects it to God's *kingdom* (*basileia* 2:5), in which both rich and poor are equal members. See Allison, *James*, 402; Davids, *The Epistle of James*, 114; Moo, *The Letter of James*, 111–112; Blomberg, *James*, 116. The term "law" occurs five times in 2:8–13, half of its occurrence in the entire book of James.
13. James uses a first-class condition in Greek which presents the event as a reality.
14. The Greek is literally that they were "working sin," which contrasts with their calling "to work righteousness" (1:20).
15. James places the word "lawbreaker" at the end of the Greek sentence for emphasis.

2:8–9	2:10	2:11
Keep the royal law	*Keep the whole law*	*Do not commit adultery*
but if you show favoritism	*yet stumbles at just one point*	*but do commit murder*
you sin and are convicted by the law as lawbreakers	*is guilty of breaking all of it*	*you have become a lawbreaker*

James is clearly referring to the Ten Commandments when he mentions adultery and murder. Favoritism often goes hand in hand with oppression, and oppression is often associated either directly or indirectly with murder. Adultery is also a sign of favoritism, because perpetrators favor their own desires rather than the well-being of their spouses and families. Adultery also symbolizes unfaithfulness to God (see Ezek 23:37) – which is exactly what those who show favoritism are doing when they put their own interests ahead of God's command.

James clearly believes that the Ten Commandments and other elements of the law of Moses (like Lev 19:18) are still relevant to Christians. Yet, there are some today who dismiss the OT. James would disagree. He holds up the royal law given to Israel through Moses and shows that it applies to all who have now come to share in God's kingdom. In this, he agrees with Jesus, who said that he had not come to abolish the law but to fulfill it (Matt 5:17–20). The command given in Leviticus and repeated by Jesus, "You are to love your neighbor as yourself" still applies to us, and if we break it in any way, even by showing favoritism, we are breaking God's law.

A Chinese proverb says, "A wrong thought will result in all kinds of wrong behaviors. We should guard against it just as carefully as we would make sure that there is not even a pinhole in an air-filled lifebuoy." This proverb captures the essence of James's exhortation: *partiality*, which might seem merely a matter of personal preference, is a sin. Those who practice it are lawbreakers.

FAVORITISM

The Scriptures record several cases of favoritism, without condoning it. Genesis 37:3–4, for example, depicts Jacob's preferential treatment of Joseph. Genesis 43:34 states that Joseph favored Benjamin over his other brothers. Sarah naturally sided with her son, Isaac, over against Ishmael, her maid's son (Gen 21:9–15). Isaac favored Esau and Rebekah favored Jacob (Gen 25:28). Elkanah too favored Hannah, even though she was barren (1 Sam 1:4–5). In all these cases, favoritism resulted in suffering for all concerned.

We know from our own experience that favoritism almost inevitably hurts people, and that it affects our daily lives on many different levels. That is why both James and Paul warn Christians not to show favoritism (2:1–9; 1 Tim 5:21). Favoritism was explicitly prohibited in the Old Testament (Lev 19:15; Deut 1:17; Prov 24:23; Mal 2:9). It is sinful because it is incongruent with God's character (2 Chr 19:6–7; Job 34:19; Acts 10:34; Rom 2:11; Gal 3:27–28; Col 3:25).

To fully understand the implications of James's teaching, we must examine the destructive results of favoritism in a community or organization as well as its effect on a personal level. In Asia, favoritism frequently rears its ugly head in the form of *cronyism* – appointing friends, family members, and associates to places of authority despite their lack of qualifications for the post. This stems from the high value that Asian cultures tend to place on personal relationships. Although an emphasis on personal relationships is something positive, it may lead to misuse of power, resulting in favoritism. So, James's reprimand about giving special attention to a certain group of people challenges Christians to re-examine cronyism.

Cronyism is not found only in the business and political communities, but also shows up in the church. Faith in Christ and unity in Christ's love are the foundations of Christian community (Eph 4:4–6). Cronyism, however, destroys unity by creating distrust. Where cronyism is present, church leaders risk loss of credibility.

The people who constitute the body of Christ come from a variety of different social, ethnic, and economic groups. A sense of fairness is key in such a diverse community. We need to keep reminding ourselves that all believers are equal in Christ (Gal 3:28), although God has given individuals different gifts to help the church function effectively (1 Cor 12:4–6).

When Christian organizations ignore believers' equality in Christ and their unique spiritual gifts, their effectiveness in ministry is hindered.

By ignoring James's warning regarding favoritism and allowing cronyism, they give Satan a foothold within the organization.

Since unfair treatment marginalizes people and demeans their value, favoritism or cronyism affects people's self-worth and self-esteem. This is true both for those who are denied favor and those who enjoy it. Favoritism always undermines identity and affects the emotional and psychological health of both the victims and the beneficiaries. We see this in families, where those favored by their parents may experience resentment and ill-feeling from other family members. In churches and Christian organizations, those who are victims of cronyism may withdraw from ministry, or may not be motivated to do their work well.

In their dealings with others, Christians are called to show the wisdom that comes from God, who is impartial, loving, and merciful (Jas 3:17; 1 Pet 1:17). So Christians, and Christian communities, must exemplify God's love in the way they evaluate and value other human beings (Rom 2:1–4). Any form of favoritism, including cronyism, is contrary to God's essence and to our call to be his children.

Hyejeong Justine Han

2:12–13 Consequence of Disobeying the Royal Law

James concludes this section with a simple command: "Speak and act as those who are going to be judged by the law that gives freedom" (2:12).[16] Speech and actions together cover the broad range of human activities addressed by the law, which judges impartially.[17]

James's assertion that the law will judge every speech and action can seem disturbing, as well as constraining. But we should not forget that the law exonerates those who obey it, as well as accusing those who disobey. As Paul says, "To those who by persistence in doing good seek glory, honor and immortality, [God] will give eternal life. But for those who are self-seeking and who reject the truth and follow evil, there will be wrath and anger" (Rom 2:7–8).

James repeatedly emphasizes the freedom or liberty the law brings to those who obey it (1:25; 2:12). He does not want his listeners to live in fear of the

---

16. These verses (2:12–13) form the conclusion for both 2:8–11 and 2:1–11.
17. James asserted the certainty of the coming judgment by using the word *mellein* "about to come."

law; instead, he wants them to keep on obeying it so that they will enjoy life and liberty.

The OT law insists on proportionate punishment – life for life, eye for eye, tooth for tooth, hand for hand, foot for foot (Deut 19:21; Lev 24:20).[18] James applies this principle to attitudes too: "Judgment without mercy will be shown to anyone who has not been merciful" (2:13a). Those who spurn the poor while fawning on the rich are most certainly not showing mercy, and have no grounds for expecting to receive the mercy they did not extend to others.

Our Lord Jesus Christ encouraged his followers to show mercy: "You have heard that it was said, 'Eye for eye, and tooth for tooth.' But I tell you, do not resist an evil person. If anyone slaps you on the right cheek, turn to them the other cheek also" (Matt 5:38–39).[19] He also told them to "be merciful, just as your Father is merciful" (Luke 6:36). So, James concludes: "Mercy triumphs over judgment" (2:13b). When believers are merciful to others, they will triumph over any judgment the law might impose on them.

God is an impartial judge, who is not swayed by human wealth or poverty (Eph 6:8; Col 3:24–25; Heb 11:6). He will judge us by the same standards we have applied to others and will uphold his just and holy law. But God is also full of mercy and grace toward those who love him. When believers show mercy in what they say and do, the law of liberty delivers them from condemnation.

Although the Lord is gracious and merciful, we should not put his mercy to the test as the unmerciful servant did in Jesus's parable in Matthew 18:21–35. That servant was shown mercy and forgiven his debt, but refused to show the same mercy to a servant who owed him money. As a result, he lost even the mercy that had been shown to him.

2:14–26 FAITH AND WORKS

Immediately after Jesus had affirmed the command to "love your neighbor as yourself" (Luke 10:27, quoting Lev 19:18), a teacher of the law wanted to know who his neighbor was. The Lord Jesus told the following story, which concluded with a question for the teacher:

---

18. The New Testament often refers to this principle (Matt 5:38–39; 7:1–2; 10:32–33; 16:27; 1 Cor 3:17; 14:38; 16:22).
19. See also Luke 6:36 for the exhortation to be merciful as God himself is merciful. The Jewish sage Ben Sira has a similar saying: "If one has no mercy toward another like himself, can he then seek pardon for his own sins?" (Sirach 28:4).

"A man was going down from Jerusalem to Jericho, when he was attacked by robbers. They stripped him of his clothes, beat him and went away, leaving him half dead. A priest happened to be going down the same road, and when he saw the man, he passed by on the other side. So too, a Levite, when he came to the place and saw him, passed by on the other side. But a Samaritan, as he traveled, came where the man was; and when he saw him, he took pity on him. He went to him and bandaged his wounds, pouring on oil and wine. Then he put the man on his own donkey, brought him to an inn and took care of him. The next day he took out two denarii and gave them to the innkeeper. 'Look after him,' he said, 'and when I return, I will reimburse you for any extra expense you may have.'"

"Which of these three do you think was a neighbor to the man who fell into the hands of robbers?"

The expert in the law replied, "The one who had mercy on him." (Luke 10:30–37a)

James does not want his readers to be like the priest or the Levite, "spiritual" men who failed to care for the wounded man. Instead, James wants them to demonstrate their faith with deeds of kindness and mercy, which are a vital part of their faith. But he knows that some of his readers will object to what he is saying, and so he takes times to explain what he means when he says that "faith by itself, if it not accompanied by action, is dead" (2:17).

This second half of the chapter is related to the first half by the references to judgment (2:12–13) and salvation (2:14, 16), by the call to exercise mercy (2:13) by providing for those in need (2:15–16), and by its emphasis on doing right (2:8, 19) and working together (2:8, 22).

2:14 Crucial Questions

In 2:1–13 James speaks in practical terms about what believers should *not* do (they should not show favoritism). Now, in equally practical terms, he is going to address the question of what they should do: they should rush to help the needy (2:14–17). Faith is not passive; it is action oriented. As before, James introduces this new topic by referring to his readers as his "brothers and sisters" (2:14a). Although he is rebuking them, he does so with gentleness, as a caring and committed family member.

Before giving his next example, James wants his readers to start thinking about the relationship between faith and deeds. He touched on this in the prologue when he spoke about what constitutes true religion (1:27), but now he wants to explore it in more depth. So he asks two rhetorical questions: "What good is it, my brothers and sisters, if someone claims to have faith but has no deeds? Can such faith save them?" (2:14).

The "faith" James is referring to is faith in Christ (see 2:1). So, is James saying that those who have faith in Christ but no deeds cannot be saved? To answer that question, we have to look at the context. In the preceding verses, James was discussing partiality and saying that judgment will come on those whose words and actions transgress God's royal law (2:12–13). Given this context, the word "save" can be understood as meaning "provide an excuse." In other words, what James is saying is, "Does having faith in Christ *excuse* believers from the obligation to obey the royal law? Can they simply ignore it?" The answer is clearly "No." Christians will be found guilty and judged when they sin. This judgment may be in the future, or it may come in the present, when their sin is exposed.

Some readers have thought that James's teachings about the need to obey the law contradict Paul's teaching. After all, Paul says that Christians have "died to the law" (Rom 7:4a) and warns that "you who are trying to be justified by the law have been alienated from Christ; you have fallen away from grace" (Gal 5:4). He stresses that we are saved by grace as a gift of God, "not by works, so that no one can boast" (Eph 2:9). So is Paul suggesting that Christians do not need to keep the law? Once again, we need to look at the context in which Paul was writing. He was responding to people who were saying that for anyone to be saved they had to observe all the rituals of the Jewish law, including observing Jewish festivals like the Passover and circumcising their sons. They thought that doing these things was necessary to earn salvation. But neither Paul nor James believed that one has to keep the law of Moses in order to earn salvation. Both stress the generosity of God as one who gives freely.

Paul and James also agree that once a person is saved, the law gives guidance on how to live a Christian life. For example, Paul upholds the commandment "Do not steal," when he says, "Anyone who has been stealing must steal no longer, but must work, doing something useful with their own hands, that they may have something to share with those in need" (Eph 4:28) and the commandment, "Honor your father and your mother," when he writes, "Children, obey your parents in everything, for this pleases the Lord" (Col 3:20).

So while we are not saved by observing the law, once we have received salvation and become members of God's kingdom, we obey his perfect law out of gratitude for his amazing grace.

2:15–16 Faith and the Needy

Failure to obey the royal law can take the form of discriminating against the poor and favoring the rich, but it can also take the form of neglect, as in the next example James gives: "Suppose a brother or a sister is without clothes and daily food. If one of you says to them, 'Go in peace; keep warm and well fed,' but does nothing about their physical needs, what good is it?" (2:15–16).[20] Today, a believer might say, "I'll pray for you," instead of helping someone who is in desperate need of the basic necessities of food and clothing. James wants the believers to act to meet needs, not merely utter a blessing or pray for them.

James would have known how the early church cared for its needy members (Acts 6:1–6). He would have witnessed the great famine in Judah in 44–48 AD and known that the Apostle Paul had not been content merely to pray for the believers there, but had sprung into action and collected money from the churches to take to his suffering brothers and sisters (Acts 11:27–30; 24:17; Rom 15:26; Gal 2:10). James wanted his readers to behave like that, rather than merely wishing the suffering good luck: "Go in peace; keep warm and well fed."[21]

Genuine faith takes action. Like the apostles and other believers in the early church, we should be committed to helping the poor. Just as in James's day, many people today are in need of food and clothing – think of the homeless, the destitute, refugees. God, his law, and James demand that we are not satisfied just to pray for those in need; we must also help them. Faith proves itself in concrete acts and sacrificial service.

Elsewhere in this letter, James has simply used the word "brothers" (which the NIV rightly translates as "brothers and sisters"). However, when speaking about the needy in 2:15, he specifically uses the word "sister" (2:15). He was well aware of the plight of widows and abandoned wives, and how they struggled to survive. The church in Jerusalem had even appointed seven deacons to minister to them (Acts 6:1–6).

In many parts of Asia, there are still many needy men and women. Christians cannot simply wish them well or pray for them. Instead, they must take care of their needs. Faith springs into action and provides for the needy. If we just wish them well, James would say to us: "No, there is no good in

---

20. The Greek construction (a third-class condition) envisions the possibility of someone actually proposing this argument.
21. "Go in peace" was a common way of saying goodbye to someone (Exod 4:18; Judg 18:6; 1 Sam 1:17; 20:42; 29:7; 2 Kgs 5:19; Luke 7:50; 8:48; 24:36; John 20:19; Acts 16:36).

claiming to have faith if you do not have any deeds of kindness. No, your faith in Christ without deeds of kindness will not deliver you from judgment under the law." As believers in Christ, we are to obey the royal law and provide the necessities of life to those who need them. Our faith should drive us to action without demanding anything in return, not even gratitude. We should give knowing that whatever we do for one of his little ones, we do for Jesus (Matt 25:31–46). Such giving will not earn us salvation, but it will protect us from the accusation that we have violated the royal law.

2:17 The Key Message

James concludes this discussion by summarizing his key message: "Faith by itself, if it is not accompanied by action, is dead" (2:17). The word "dead" in this context means "useless." When believers claim to have faith in God but don't actively help those in need, their faith is useless – they are neither living in dependence on God nor bearing testimony to God's generosity. Faith, when it demonstrates itself through works, is a powerful testimony to God's provision through God's people.

If someone says, "I am a believer," but shows partiality to the rich and doesn't provide for the needs of the poor, we can rightly be suspicious about the genuineness of their faith. James expands on this key message in the following verses (2:18–25) before repeating his conclusion: "As the body without the spirit is dead, so faith without deeds is dead" (2:26).

2:18–26 Response to Objections

Writers in antiquity often used imaginary opponents to make arguments. The imaginary opponent would object to the writer's original statement, and the writer would respond with a counter-argument. Paul, for example, addresses an imaginary opponent when he writes, "One of you will say to me: 'Then why does God still blame us? For who is able to resist his will?'" (Rom 9:19). James does the same as he responds to those who object to the point he is making.

2:18–20 The argument

Since ancient Greek did not make much use of punctuation marks, scholars disagree about exactly how this imaginary argument should be read.[22] The NIV translates it as "You have faith; I have deeds" (2:18). But, more likely, it

---

22. The complexity is reflected in the English translations. Subdividing the verse into sections helps us see how translations divide: [A] "But if someone will say" [B] "You have faith" [C] "And I have works," and [D] "Show me your faith without works and I'll show you

should be punctuated like this: "Do you have faith?" "I have works." In other words, the imaginary opponent was asking a question that showed that he assumed that some people have faith (without works) while others have works (without faith).

James responds: "Show me your faith without deeds, and I will show you my faith by my deeds" (2:18b). He is challenging his opponent to show how faith functions in real life if it does not affect what one does. Anyone can claim to have faith, but unless that faith has real consequences for how one lives, that faith is dead or useless. Faith must express itself in works; otherwise, it is not *biblical faith*.[23]

To ram home his point, James uses an illustration to show that a mere claim to have faith is not enough. "You believe that there is one God. Good! Even the demons believe that – and shudder" (2:19). Jewish believers recited and believed the *Shema* (Deut 6:4–6): "Hear, O Israel: The LORD our God, the LORD is one." James fully agreed with this statement. But so would demons! They know there is only one true God – and they fear him.[24] But the demons' faith has no effect on their behavior, and it does not save them. In the same way, if believers claim that they have faith but do not show it in actions such as caring for the poor, then all they have is a lifeless faith.

These days, many call themselves Christians or acknowledge the greatness of Christ, but their faith does not affect how they live. Such faith is as useless as the "faith" of demons. It is mere mental assent, not heartfelt biblical faith.

Having shown the emptiness of his opponent's arguments, James addresses the person directly as "you foolish person" (2:20a). Literally, what he says is "you empty person." The same word is translated "empty-handed" in Mark 12:3. James is challenging his opponents to think more clearly. Since they were sending away needy people empty-handed, James thinks it fair to call them empty-headed – they have an empty faith.

Then he asks them, "Do you want evidence that faith without deeds is useless?" (2:20b). The word "useless" is a synonym for "empty."[25] He offers his

---

my faith through works." The NJB and KJV, for example, consider [B] [C] and [D] as objector's arguments, whereas the NIV, ESV, NRSV, and NLT consider only [B] and [C] as the objector's arguments.

23. See Robert Y. K. Fung, "Justification in the Epistle of James," in *Right with God: Justification in the Bible and the World*, ed. D. A. Carson (Grand Rapids: Baker, 1992), 148–151.

24. The verb *shudder* is a *hapax* (a word that occurs only one time) in the NT. However, it is used twice in the ancient Greek translation of the OT (Job 4:15; Jer 2:12). In Jeremiah, the context is idolatry.

25. There is a play on words here since "useless" (*argē*) and "works" (*arga*) sound similar in Greek and are morphologically related.

empty-headed opponents two biblical examples that prove that a faith without works is an empty faith.

2:21–24 The example of Abraham

James's first example is Abraham, whom the Jews revered as the father of their race and the founder of their religion. Two ancient Jewish writers, Philo and Josephus, regarded Abraham as the first person to assert that there was only one God.[26] Philo also described him as an ordinary man who was victorious over his passions and so achieved perfection.[27] In full awareness of Abraham's status, James cites him as an example of the relationship between faith and works.

James begins by asking a question that his Jewish readers would immediately have answered affirmatively: "Was not our father Abraham considered righteous for what he did when he offered his son Isaac on the altar?" (2:21; see Gen 22).[28] According to Jewish tradition, by being willing to offer Isaac as a sacrifice, Abraham passed God's ultimate test of faith.

To emphasize his point, James reiterates it: "You see that his faith and his actions were working together, and his faith was made complete by what he did" (2:22). Abraham's faith became mature (was completed) when he was willing to act on his faith. His faith and works went hand in hand.[29]

Because of his actions, Abraham received the highest possible honor in an honor-based culture in that he was acknowledged as a righteous person (2:22a). It was an honor he shared with Noah (Gen 6:9) and David (1 Kgs 3:6). God himself declared Abraham righteous because his faith proved itself in action. In addition, Abraham received a very special designation: "God's friend" (2:23; see also 2 Chr 20:7; Isa 41:8).[30] Only one other person in the history of Israel received that title, namely, Moses (Exod 33:11). Abraham attained that privileged status because he combined faith with works.[31] James wants his readers to know that faith accompanied by works receives the highest commendation from God.

James concludes the example of Abraham with a simple statement: "You see that a person is considered righteous by what they do and not by faith

---

26. Philo, *On the Virtues*, XXXIX, 216; Josephus, *Jewish Antiquities,* 1.155.
27. Philo, *On the Life of Abraham*, 10.48–50.
28. James's words reflect the Septuagint translation rather than the Masoretic text.
29. James uses the imperfect tense that indicates that Abraham's faith *actively* collaborated with his works.
30. Later, James contrasts being God's friend (2:23) and the world's friend (4:4).
31. The Jewish Hellenistic writer Philo also affirmed that Abraham received this privileged title when he offered his son on the altar (Philo, *Abraham,* 32.170).

alone" (2:24). As in 2:22, he begins with the words, "you see." He wants his readers to see this point for themselves. Faith is alive when it follows through with action.

2:25 The example of Rahab

Some people might argue that Abraham was too great to be an example for ordinary people. So, James's second example involves someone very different. Abraham was a man; Rahab was a woman.[32] He was the founder of the Jewish nation; she was a Canaanite, a member of a group that was hostile to the Jews. He was a moral leader; she was a prostitute. Yet, she shared Abraham's faith in the uniqueness of YHWH God (Josh 2:11).[33] Her faith led her to protect the spies whom Joshua sent, despite knowing that if she were caught she would be executed. Because of her faith, God protected her, and Joshua's army spared Rahab and her family (Josh 6:22–25).

James introduces Rahab with the words "in the same way," indicating that she and Abraham were very similar when it came to putting faith into action (2:25). God considered them both "righteous" because of their faith in action. This point becomes clear when we look at the parallelism in these verses:

2:21	Abraham was considered righteous . . . when he offered his son Isaac
2:24	A person is considered righteous by what they do and not by faith alone
2:25	Rahab was considered righteous . . . when she gave lodging to the spies

2:26 The body metaphor

The examples of Abraham and Rahab should be enough to convince the readers that faith needs to be authenticated by works. But James adds one more metaphor to complete his argument: "As the body without the spirit is dead, so faith without deeds is dead" (2:26).

A human body is alive and moves around as long as it has a living spirit within it. But when the spirit leaves, the body is dead and doesn't move. In the same way, a faith that isn't animated by works is dead. And being "dead" is even worse than being "useless" (2:20)!

Jesus himself made this point:

---

32. It is possible James chose to use the example of a man and a woman since he had earlier mentioned both a brother and a sister in need (2:15).
33. Her words resemble Moses's words in Deuteronomy 4:39.

When the Son of Man comes in his glory, and all the angels with him, he will sit on his glorious throne. All the nations will be gathered before him, and he will separate the people one from another as a shepherd separates the sheep from the goats. He will put the sheep on his right and the goats on his left.

Then the King will say to those on his right, "Come, you who are blessed by my Father; take your inheritance, the kingdom prepared for you since the creation of the world. For I was hungry and you gave me something to eat, I was thirsty and you gave me something to drink, I was a stranger and you invited me in, I needed clothes and you clothed me, I was sick and you looked after me, I was in prison and you came to visit me."

Then the righteous will answer him, "Lord, when did we see you hungry and feed you, or thirsty and give you something to drink? When did we see you a stranger and invite you in, or needing clothes and clothe you? When did we see you sick or in prison and go to visit you?"

The King will reply, "Truly I tell you, whatever you did for one of the least of these brothers and sisters of mine, you did for me." (Matt 25:31–40)

Both James and Jesus speak of concrete actions: helping the poor, the hungry, and those suffering. Clearly, God expects our claim to have faith to be accompanied by deeds of mercy, the kind of deeds that James has been pleading for in 1:27–2:16.

James's exhortation has great relevance for those of us living in Asia today. What are *we* doing for the hungry, the poor, and the suffering? Our faith in God must show itself in sharing our material resources and blessings with those in need. We must be sensitive to situations where the rich are favored and the poor oppressed, and work tirelessly to counter such injustice – while at the same time checking our own hearts to make sure that we are not guilty of favoring the rich and looking down on the poor. Our faith in Christ should drive us to action.

JAMES AND PAUL

How can James say that Christians are justified by works along with faith (Jas 2:24), while Paul says that they are justified by faith apart from works (Rom 3:28)? Is this not a contradiction? To understand what is going on, we need to understand how each of these writers use the Greek word *dikaióo* (translated "justified" in English), how each one employs the example of Abraham, and the particular situation that each writer was addressing.

Dikaióo. Both Paul and James use the word *dikaióo* in a legal sense, but each focuses on a different aspect of its meaning. Paul focuses on it as a judge's verdict, whereby someone is officially declared to be legally righteous. He insists that this is not a verdict one can earn by what one does: "No one will be declared righteous in God's sight by the works of the law; rather, through the law we become conscious of our sin . . . This righteousness is given through faith in Jesus Christ to all who believe" (Rom 3:20, 22). A believer's status as righteous is thus "the gift of God" rather than something one deserves because of one's good works (Eph 2:8–9). James, on the other hand, is concerned with the result of what God has done, and stresses the need for visible proof that one has been declared righteous. For example, he writes, "Show me your faith without deeds, and I will show you my faith by my deeds" (Jas 2:18). Paul would concur: "It is not those who hear the law who are righteous in God's sight, but it is those who obey the law who will be declared righteous" (Rom 2:13). To sum up: Paul is speaking about *how* a person is saved (by faith alone) while James is speaking about how someone *shows* that they have been saved.

The example of Abraham. Both Paul and James use the example of Abraham to support their case. Paul points to Genesis 15:1–6 (where the childless Abraham believed God's promise that he would have innumerable descendants) to show that God justified Abraham solely because he had faith (Rom 4:1–3). He argues that this example explains how we too can be declared legally righteous solely because we have faith in what Christ has done, rather than because of anything we have done. James, however, refers to an incident much later in Abraham's life, when he was asked to sacrifice his only son, Isaac, who had been born as a result of the promise in the passage Paul referred to (Gen 22:1–19). Abraham's obedience is evidence that his righteousness was genuine and had matured. Paul would concur that righteousness leads to obedience. In Romans 6 he insists that those who have true faith will demonstrate it by living transformed lives, fleeing from sin and pursuing holiness. To sum up: Believers are saved by faith alone, but that faith is never alone – it must result in appropriate actions.

Particular context. Paul's teaching on justification by faith rather than works was seized on by some as an excuse to go on sinning (Rom 6:1). They claimed that the more they sinned, the more God's grace flowed, and that was a good thing! Others may have said that they did not need to do good works or live a moral life because all that mattered was having faith. In his letter, James may well be trying to correct this false and distorted interpretation and application of Paul's doctrine of justification. Paul himself was horrified by this caricature of faith and would have agreed with the point James is making.

When properly read, and understood in context, James and Paul come together like two sides of the same coin. Together, they provide a complementary and comprehensive understanding of what it truly means to put our trust in and be transformed by our Lord and Savior Jesus Christ.

Lewis Winkler

JAMES 3:1–18

MATURITY IN SPEECH AND WISDOM

An Indian saying goes: "Even a frog endangers itself when it opens its mouth." During the rainy season, frogs croak to announce their presence to potential mates. Cobras and other snakes hear the croaking, follow the sound, and eat the frogs. Indian parents repeat this saying to their children, in order to remind them to be careful in their speech.

In his prologue, James advised believers to pray for wisdom (1:5), to be slow to speak (1:19), and to keep a tight rein on their tongues (1:26). Now he expands on these principles. These instructions are not about trivial matters; they are key elements of spiritual maturity.

Just as the Lord Jesus said, our words reflect our inner being, our hearts (Luke 6:45). Our desires arouse jealousy, anger, pride, greed, slander, lies, gossip, insults, grumbling, boasting and all kinds of evil speech. So, James begins by warning against untamed tongues.

3:1–12 MATURE SPEECH

James roots his teachings firmly in the wisdom tradition. He would have known many proverbs that offered cautions about one's speech:

"The words of the reckless pierce like swords, but the tongue of the wise brings healing." (Prov 12:18)

"Those who guard their lips preserve their lives, but those who speak rashly will come to ruin." (Prov 13:3)

"The tongue of the wise adorns knowledge, but the mouth of the fool gushes folly." (Prov 15:2)

"The soothing tongue is a tree of life, but a perverse tongue crushes the spirit." (Prov 15:4)

"The tongue has the power of life and death." (Prov 18:21a)

The Chinese, too, have similar proverbs: "When words are many, there may be error," "Disease comes in through our mouth; calamity comes out of our mouth," and "Vain promises bring disaster." Given all these warnings, it is hardly surprising that James begins his section on speech with warnings against desiring a position that requires us to talk!

3:1–2a Warning to Teachers

Ancient cultures honored teachers. Since most people were uneducated laborers, who lacked the time and the literacy to study and teach the truths of God, they looked up to teachers. In Jewish culture, the task of teaching was generally reserved for priests, rabbis, and teachers of the law, who were deeply respected.[1] This tradition continued in the NT church, where teachers are referred to in the same breath as prophets and apostles (Acts 13:1; 1 Cor 12:28–29; Eph 4:11). Clearly, being a teacher was an attractive option for anyone seeking prestige, honor, or financial gain.

James himself was a respected leader and teacher (Gal 2:9; Acts 15:13). Yet he warns his readers, "not many of you should become teachers" (3:1).[2] He does not do this because he is trying to protect his position. Rather, he wants them to be cautious about assuming leadership because of the risks involved: "we who teach will be judged more strictly" (3:1). Christians should not lightly decide to take up teaching.

With great calling comes great responsibility. Teachers influence both by their lips and by their lives. So they must live up to the standards they lay down for others. Paul says, "You . . . have no excuse, you who pass judgment on someone else, for at whatever point you judge another, you are condemning yourself" (Rom 2:1). When teachers fail to live up to the standards they teach, they are condemned by their own words. They cannot plead ignorance of the law, and so, they will be judged more strictly than their disciples or students.

James acknowledges how difficult it is for of anyone (including himself) to achieve such high standards: "We all stumble in many ways" (3:2a). Although the word "stumble" usually refers to moral failing,[3] James here links it with speech: "Anyone who [never stumbles] in what they say is perfect, able to keep their whole body in check" (3:2b). "Keep in check" is the same metaphor as "keep a tight rein" (1:26). In both places James is warning his readers to carefully control their speech (see also 3:3).

Controlling one's tongue is so difficult that if someone never stumbles in what they say, then they are perfect, fully mature, and able to exercise

---

1. In the Gospels, Jesus is often referred to as a teacher and sometimes addressed as "rabbi."

2. In this instance, the "fellow believers" (literally, "brothers") were most likely men, since very few women were teachers, especially in Greek culture. Jewish mothers were entrusted with teaching their children and helpers at home. Here, too, the word "brothers" introduces a new section (see also 3:10; 3:12).

3. This word for "stumble" (*ptaiein*) occurs only five times in the NT, and three of those occurrences are in this letter (twice here and another time in 2:10).

self-control in all other matters too.[4] If we can control our speech – neither speak too soon nor say something we should not say – we will also be able to control the evil desires that lure us into other sins (1:14–15).

Teachers do a lot of talking. They speak to communicate the content being taught, to control the group they are teaching, and to guide individuals within a class or a counseling session. In all these instances, they can stumble by teaching something wrong or by not living up to what they teach. They can stumble by abusing their position of power in relation to a class. They can stumble by uttering harsh words to an individual – as the Chinese say, "A sharp tongue or pen can kill without a knife." They can even stumble by refusing to admit the possibility that they have made a mistake, covering it up for fear of losing face. There are plenty of opportunities for teachers' words to trip them up! So, James is concerned that teachers learn to control their tongues. Once they can do this, they can control all their behavior.

We in Asia must heed James's warning all the more because of the great respect teachers enjoy in our part of the world. In schools and colleges, students stand when a teacher enters the class and wait until the teacher tells them to sit down. Teachers are always addressed as "sir," "teacher," "madam," or "miss" – and never by their first name as in the West. Students sometimes bow to teachers when they pass them in the halls, streets, and even markets. These same gestures of respect are shown to Christian leaders and teachers – and may motivate some people to become teachers. They are less interested in sharing knowledge or wisdom than in enjoying the prestige associated with a teaching position.

When we feel this temptation, we need to heed James warning and pair it with his later words: "Who is wise and understanding among you? Let them show it by their good life, by deeds done in the humility that comes from wisdom" (3:13). One should enter a leadership or teaching position carefully and then lead with godly wisdom, a good life, and actions done in humility. One should not strive to be a teacher or church leader for the wrong motives.

All of us who teach in Asia (whether in schools, universities, churches, mission organizations, or theological institutions) must guard our speech and do nothing that will bring ourselves or our teaching into disrepute. Our strongest asset, our tongue, is also our most dangerous stumbling block.

---

4. James uses a first-class conditional in 3:2, expressing that this premise is true for the sake of the argument.

3:3–8 Danger in Speech

Speech is powerful; it can yield wonderful or terrible results. As an ancient Chinese proverb says, "The tongue is like a sharp knife; it kills without drawing blood." M. Luzzatto, an eighteenth-century rabbi, quoted Jewish scholars as saying that damaging speech is equivalent to killing three people: "It destroys the reputation of the victim, damages the perceptions of the listener, and diminishes the standing of the speaker."[5] Evil speech not only harms individuals but scars entire communities and churches.

James uses a series of vivid metaphors to illustrate the power of the tongue. As we read them, we would do well to remember that these days we communicate not only through spoken words but also in writing. So we should reflect on how James's warnings apply to how we use words in our emails, tweets, texts, and other social media.

3:3 A horse and a bit

James's first metaphor follows on from his earlier reference to keeping the tongue on a "tight rein" (1:26; see also 3:2). In James's day, horses were ridden by army officers and by couriers who carried important messages across the Roman Empire in an early form of mail service. The rider used reins attached to a metal "bit" placed inside the horse's mouth to control the horse's movements. When the rider wanted to change direction, he would pull on the reins, the hard bit would press against the soft flesh inside the horse's mouth, and the horse would change direction in order to relieve the discomfort. That is the image James has in mind when he says, "When we put bits in the mouths of horses to make them obey us, we can turn the whole animal" (3:3). James's readers knew that the presence of a small bit was enough to compel the obedience of a powerful, strong-willed horse. In the same way the tongue – also a small object in the mouth – can direct a person's course either along a path of righteousness or down a path of destruction.

3:4 A ship and its rudder

Next James uses the metaphor of a ship's rudder.[6] In his day, sailors relied on wind in a ship's sails to move it across the sea, while they steered with a rudder (3:4). A rudder is simply a small piece of wood or metal extending into the

---

5. Cited by A. Morinis, *Climbing Jacob's Ladder* (Boston: Trumpeter Books, 2002), 163.
6. James begins 3:4 with the word "behold" (*idou*) – a Hebrew expression intended to draw attention to something (see also 3:5; 5:4, 7, 9). This word is not translated in the NIV.

water at the back of the ship. Adjusting the angle of the rudder changes the direction in which the ship is moving.

A rudder is very small compared to the ship it steers. The rudder of the *Titanic*, for example, was 24 meters high, 4.6 meters wide, and weighted 100 tons. In other words, it was roughly the size and weight of two shipping containers. But this relatively small rudder could steer a ship that was 270 meters long and weighed some 50,000 tons.

James points out that a small rudder is enough to counter the effects of strong winds and steer the ship "wherever the pilot wants to go."[7] Similarly, our tongue, although only two to three inches long and weighing only seventy to eighty grams, is extremely powerful. It can direct us away from humility and onto the rocks of pride as it makes "great boasts." As experience has shown, the words people speak can have disastrous consequences for their whole life.[8]

Unfortunately, teachers' tongues can also make great boasts, for we may be prone to exaggerate our knowledge and our own importance. The Lord Jesus noticed this and commented, "[Some teachers] love the place of honor at banquets and the most important seats in the synagogues; they love to be greeted with respect in the marketplaces and to be called 'Rabbi' by others" (Matt 23:6–7). Jesus warned his followers that they should not be like this, and James is repeating that warning.

3:5–6 A spark and a wildfire

Small sparks from a campfire or a discarded cigarette butt can start vast forest fires. In recent years, such fires have rolled across parts of Australia, the USA, Canada, France, Spain and Greece, destroying lives and property.[9] We can easily understand what James means when he says, "Consider what a great forest is set on fire by a small spark" (3:5b).[10]

---

7. The Greek word translated "pilot" means "one who leads the ship in a straight path."
8. Luke Johnson speaks of "the guiding desire (the steersman), the means of control (the rudder), and that which is controlled (the ship), corresponding in turn to human desire, the tongue, and the body." *The Letter of James*, AYBC, 37A (New York: Doubleday, 1995), 258.
9. It has been estimated that in the United States and Australia, cigarette butts start 20% of all fires and cause billions of dollars in property damage. Max Tawadrous, "Cigarettes: How Often They Cause Fires?" *Fire Investigations* (May 2000): 1; Marde Hoy and Stephen Morton, "Deaths Associated with Fires Caused by Cigarettes," *Victorian Institute of Forensic Medicine* (October 2006): 7.
10. This verse too starts with "behold" (*idou*). James makes a contrast between the *great* fire and the *small* spark.

Just as a fire can devour everything in its path, so careless words can destroy a person's life.[11] As James says, "The tongue also is a fire, a world of evil among the parts of the body. It corrupts the whole body, sets the whole course of one's life on fire, and is itself set on fire by hell" (3:6). Here he is reflecting the wisdom found in the book of Proverbs: "A scoundrel plots evil, and on their lips it is like a scorching fire" (Prov 16:27).[12]

Since the tongue "sets on fire the entire course of ones' life," it is appropriate that it is "set on fire by hell."[13] The word translated "hell" is *Gehenna*. The literal Gehenna was a ravine south of Jerusalem that was also known as the Valley of the Sons of Hinnom (Josh 15:8; Neh 11:30). It once housed a temple where human sacrifices were offered, and so the Jews regarded it as an accursed place where the bodies of evildoers were thrown (2 Kgs 23:10; Jer 7:32–33). Thus the name Gehenna became a metaphor for a place of destruction (Matt 5:22, 29, 30; 10:28; 18:9; 23:15; Mark 9:45, 47; Luke 12:5) – an appropriate source for a tongue that spreads destruction.

This frightening image should cause us all to think very carefully before we speak, and to be wary of becoming teachers who can start conflagrations.

3:7–8 Creatures wild and tame

For the Jews, "animals, birds, reptiles and sea creatures" represented the entire animal kingdom that God had commanded people to govern and take care of (3:7, see Gen 1:20–26). Many of these creatures have indeed been tamed – horses pull carts, elephants transport goods, and bees provide honey. Snake charmers even charm cobras for people's entertainment. Yet, while the natural world can be tamed, "no human being can tame the tongue" (3:8a). This statement is not meant to drive us to despair, but to alert us to our vulnerability. We can neither let down our guard nor assume that our words will always be wise.

---

11. The phrase the NIV translates as "the whole course of one's life" was used to refer to "the wheel of origin or natural life" and so to the unending cycle of reincarnation. Given that James and the Jews did not believe in reincarnation, he is using this expression merely to refer to the ups and downs of life.
12. Ben Sira also said that the tongue "has no power over the godly; they will not be burned in its flame. Those who forsake the Lord will fall into its power; it will burn among them and will not be put out" (Sir 28:22–23a; see also Ps 120:3–4; Isa 30:27).
13. Richard J. Bauckham, "The Tongue Set on Fire by Hell [James 3:6]," in *The Fate of the Dead: Studies on the Jewish and Christian Apocalypses* (Leiden: Brill, 1998), 119–131.

Earlier, James referred to a double-minded person as "restless." Now, he applies that adjective to the untamed tongue,[14] describing it as "a restless evil" (3:8b). The metaphor suggests trouble, like a raging fire destroying land and properties or a fierce animal prowling in search of its prey. An early Christian writer echoes James's words, saying "Slander is evil; it is a restless demon, never at peace."[15] The tongue is full of evil, in contrast to our God who cannot even be tempted by evil (1:13).

The tongue is as dangerous as a cobra or an adder, for it is "full of deadly poison." In saying this, James may be remembering the psalmist's request for God to deliver him from the evildoers who "make their tongues as sharp as a serpent's; the poison of vipers is on their lips" (Ps 140:3). Words can literally be deadly since they may spark fights that lead to wars and murders.

The life of Li Lin Po, an advisor to the Emperor Tang Shzen Tzung of the Tang Dynasty (712–716 AD), illustrates the harm that the tongue can cause. He was a brilliant man who appeared to be friendly and charming, although he was actually ruthless and cunning. He used his tongue to flatter the emperor and his associates and to spread false rumors about anyone he perceived as a rival. The ancient historian Sze Ma Guang, referred to him as having "honey in his mouth" while preparing to plunge a dagger in someone's belly.

While we may not be as deliberate as Li Lin Po in using our tongues to poison someone's prospects, we all need to remember that our tongues can spread poison that is damaging to our families, our churches, and our communities. To avoid doing this, even accidentally, we must watch what we say! We need to tame our tongues so that they speak pure and righteous words.

3:9–12 Inconsistency in Speech

James knows some of his readers may already be trying to control their tongues. So he adopts a gentler tone as he addresses the inconsistency he sees among them.

3:9–10 Praising and cursing

Praising and cursing are opposites, yet both come out of the same mouth: "With the tongue we praise our Lord and Father, and with it we curse human beings, who have been made in God's likeness. Out of the same mouth come

---

14. The two words, "can tame" are alliterative (*damasai dunatai*) and a good example of James's rhetorical ability.
15. *Shepherd of Hermas*, Mandate 2.3.

praise and cursing" (3:9–10a).[16] How can one mouth produce two opposite types of speech?[17] It seems that the people doing this are not even aware that what they are doing is hypocritical.

Praising God was part of Jewish worship: "May the peoples praise you, God; may all the peoples praise you" (Ps 67:3). It was also a common response to good news: Simeon praised God when he saw the infant Jesus (Luke 2:28) and the people praised God when they saw what Jesus was doing (Luke 7:16). On the other hand, cursing was also common (Ps 35:26; Prov 30:11; Eccl 7:21–22).

But the Lord Jesus instructed his followers to "bless those who curse you, pray for those who mistreat you" (Luke 6:28). James follows the Lord's instruction and denounces cursing. His reason for why we should not curse people is rooted in creation: God created human beings in his own image (3:9b; also Gen 1:26–27). How can we curse people who are formed in the image of God whom we love and worship? To curse people while praising God is like honoring someone in their presence but spitting on their portrait when we are alone. The Chinese refer to people who act like this as "double-headed snakes."

James has a clear message for his readers who bless God while cursing people: "My brothers and sisters, this should not be" (3:10b). He then uses three metaphors to illustrate how utterly inconsistent such behavior is.

3:11 A spring of water

James's first illustration is a spring. He asks, "Can both fresh water and salt water flow from the same spring?" (3:11). Much of West Asia is a dry region where people rely on fresh-water springs for survival. Villages and cities were built around these water sources. However, the water from some springs was not fit for drinking because it was brackish and had an unpleasant taste, as the Israelites discovered at Marah (Exod 15:23). But the same spring would not produce fresh water one day and bitter water the next. In the same way, how can a believer's mouth produce sweet praises to God but also pronounce bitter curses upon people created in God's image?

3:12a A tree and its fruit

James's second illustration is a tree: "My brothers and sisters, can a fig tree bear olives, or a grapevine bear figs?" (3:12a). Figs, olives, and grapes were staple

---

16. James alternates between "tongue" and "mouth" in these verses.
17. James structures these clauses as parallel and uses the same prepositional phrase ("with it") and tense to drive home the point that these actions were exactly opposite.

crops in the region at that time. People grew them, harvested them, and ate them. So they knew that a fig tree wouldn't bear olives and that a grapevine couldn't bear figs. A tree bore only its own kind of fruit. This, too, is common sense theology, of the same kind that the Lord Jesus used when he said that false teachers could be identified by their fruit: "Do people pick grapes from thornbushes, or figs from thistles? Likewise, every good tree bears good fruit, but a bad tree bears bad fruit. A good tree cannot bear bad fruit, and a bad tree cannot bear good fruit" (Matt 7:16–18). There is something seriously wrong if the same mouth produces two different kinds of fruit: blessing God and cursing people.

3:12b Seawater

The NIV translates James's third illustration as "Neither can a salt spring produce fresh water." But the word "spring" is not in the Greek original, and more likely James is referring to seawater, which is salty. James's readers lived in towns and villages near the Mediterranean Sea, and so they would have known that seawater is unsuitable for drinking. How, then, can a "salty" mouth that produces unpleasant speech and frequently curses other people also produce refreshing speech that praises God? If someone constantly criticizes others, gossips about them, or curses them, their foul speech will pollute everything else they say, and those who hear them praise God will consider them hypocrites.

To sum up, James saw inconsistency in speech as evidence of a lack of obedience to God and a lack of love for the people who bear God's image. The Chinese proverb, "Watch someone's speech, you know their deed. Watch their deed, you know their mind," captures the essence of his teaching. One's speech gives insight into one's character. We can't praise God and curse his people. When we do that, it shows our hypocrisy.

TONGUES

The Hindu goddess Kali is often portrayed with her bloody tongue sticking out. The author Devdutt Pattanaik suggests that with the outstretched tongue, "Kali teases and mocks her devotees — she sees through their social façade and knows the dark desires they try so hard to deny or suppress."[1]

One's tongue is a window to one's physical health. A red tongue may be a sign of a vitamin deficiency, strawberry-like appearances on one's tongue may indicate Kawasaki disease, and a "hairy" tongue may harbor bacteria.[2] That is why doctors ask patients to open their mouths and show their tongues.

The Scriptures too speak of the tongue as a gauge of one's *spiritual* health. Proverb 12:18 says, "The words of the reckless pierce like swords, but the tongue of the wise brings healing." "The soothing tongue is a tree of life, but a perverse tongue crushes the spirit" (Prov 15:4). The Lord Jesus echoed this: "What goes into someone's mouth does not defile them, but what comes out of their mouth, that is what defiles them" (Matt 15:11).

James, too, depicts the tongue as a dangerous weapon. Whereas human beings have learned to steer powerful horses and mighty ships with small bits and rudders, they struggle to control their own tongue (3:3–4). Like a match or a cigarette butt that sets a forest on fire, so the tongue and its boastfulness can destroy people and their reputations (3:5). Whereas zoo keepers can tame birds, reptiles, and mammals, and marine biologists can train dolphins and whales to perform for spectators, we cannot control our tongues (3:6). The tongue is deadlier than the deadliest of snakes!

Not only is the tongue difficult to control, it is also double-sided. With one side, it praises God, but with the other side, it curses our fellow human beings who are created in God's image (3:9). This is quite contrary to nature where streams cannot produce both bitter and sweet water and figs do not grow on olive trees (3:10–12). That is why James describes the tongue as a "world of evil among the parts of the body. It corrupts the whole body, sets the whole course of one's life . . . on fire by hell" (3:6).

How do we learn to control our tongues? James — who gave the promise, "If any of you lacks wisdom, you should ask God, who gives generously to all without finding fault, and it will be given to you" (1:5) — also says, "Who is wise and understanding among you? Let them show it by their good life, *by deeds done in the humility* that comes from wisdom" (3:13; italics added). The antidote to a harmful and vicious tongue is the wisdom and humility that lead to good deeds. Such wisdom doesn't originate on earth; it originates in heaven (3:17a). And its characteristics are visible: "peace-loving, considerate, submissive, full of mercy and good fruit, impartial, and sincere" (Jas 3:17b).

If we seek this wisdom and humility, we can learn to suppress our blabber-mouth. Then, before we speak, we examine our hearts. Before we speak, we act in humility. And, before we speak, we submit and seek peace.

Modern-day "tongues" are emails, chats, blogs, tweeting, and snapchats. Each day, we witness how powerful political and religious leaders fall because of an angry email they sent or a blog they posted. James warns: "Watch your words." Instead of quickly responding to an email in anger, wait until your emotions are calm. Get someone to read your email or blog before you post it. Pray and seek God's guidance before you chat or tweet. Seek heavenly wisdom in all your correspondence. Once something is said or sent, it can't be taken back.

James concludes this section on tongues by saying, "Peacemakers who sow in peace reap a harvest of righteousness" (3:18). Whereas untamed tongues spread fire and destruction, a life of wisdom brings peace and righteousness. "The tongue has the power of life and death, and those who love it will eat its fruit" (Prov 18:21).

Andrew B. Spurgeon

1. Devdutt Pattanaik, "Kali and Her Tongue," in *India Times*, Dec 12, 2011. https://timesofindia.indiatimes.com/Kali-and-her-tongue/articleshow/10816142.cms. Accessed 11 January 2015.
2. https://health.clevelandclinic.org/what-your-tongue-can-tell-you-about-your-health/.

3:13–18 MATURE WISDOM

Since speech is so important to our lives and testimony, how can we learn to control our tongue? James deals with this question as he compares godly and ungodly wisdom (3:13–18). Wisdom from above helps us to control our tongues, whereas wisdom from below offers no help at all, and hinders and harms!

3:13 Godly Wisdom

James begins with a rhetorical question: "Who is wise and understanding among you?" (3:13a). The Jews greatly respected people with wisdom and understanding. Those were the criteria that Moses used when he instructed the people, "choose some wise, understanding and respected men from each of your tribes, and I will set them over you" (Deut 1:13). Moses assured the people that if they obeyed God's law their fame would spread among the surrounding nations, who would say, "Surely this great nation is a wise and understanding people" (Deut 4:6). Centuries later, Daniel obeyed the law and became known for his wisdom and understanding (Dan 5:11). So those who wanted to be known as teachers were probably eager to claim that they, too, were wise and understanding. James exhorts them to seek heavenly wisdom and avoid earthly wisdom.

How do we know who is truly wise? James applies a simple test: those who are wise "show it by their good life, by deeds done in the humility that comes from wisdom" (3:13b). Humble obedience to God is still the route to a reputation for wisdom, just as it was in Moses's day.

Humility is a key virtue for James, who earlier advised his readers to "humbly accept the word planted in you, which can save you" (1:21). To be humble is to have an honest view of oneself from God's perspective (that is, to see oneself as both vulnerable to sin and valuable to God) and to submit to God's authority. Humbly doing good deeds demonstrates both our faith (2:14–19) and our wisdom. Many who want a reputation as teachers and leaders forget this. Yet their students and followers will probably learn as much and more from their actions as from their words!

3:14–16 Ungodly Wisdom

Ungodly wisdom has two characteristics: bitter envy and selfish ambition. James writes, "If you harbor bitter envy and selfish ambition in your hearts, do not boast about it or deny the truth" (3:14). Leaders with godly wisdom know their worth before God and feel no need to boast about their wisdom, talents, or abilities. Nor are they envious of others' gifts and talents. They do not try to put down people; instead, they encourage others to use their talents to serve God.

Those who are merely pretending to be wise are full of "bitter envy" (3:14). Envy itself is wrong for the tenth commandment forbids it (Exod 20:17). But James adds a further dimension here when he prefixes it with the adjective, "bitter." This is the same word translated "salt water" in 3:11 – also with reference to wrong speech and emotions. Just as bitter water is unpalatable and harmful to those who drink it, so leaders and teachers who are full of "bitter envy" bring harm to their communities.

The other characteristic of unwise leaders is that their hearts are full of "selfish ambition." Ambition itself is not wrong – Paul, for example, writes, "It has always been my ambition to preach the gospel where Christ was not known" (Rom 15:20). What is wrong is the selfishness that pollutes it. The Greek philosopher Aristotle defined ambition as, "self-seeking pursuit of political office by unfair means."[18] This is the type of ambition that drives selfish politicians who want to get rich rather than to serve their communities, and so use lies and bribery to get ahead. Such leaders have no interest in helping others or in seeking the truth of a matter; they are only concerned about what will benefit them. They are the type of people Paul describes as "those who are self-seeking and who reject the truth" (Rom 2:8).

Selfishness and selfish ambition do not arise from obedience to the truth; like all evil desires, they arise from within our sinful heart (1:14–15). So James says, "If you harbor . . . selfish ambition in your hearts, do not boast about it" (3:14). Instead of boasting, we are to humble ourselves before God and his people, and seek wisdom from above.

In Indian villages where water is carried in jugs, there is a saying: "A half-filled jug splashes more water than a brim-filled jug." The villagers know that as they walk with a half-filled jug, the motion shakes the water and sets it splashing out. The English have a saying with a similar meaning: "empty vessels make the most sound." Linking these proverbs to what James is saying, those who are filled to the brim with godly wisdom have a tight rein over their mouths and can keep silent, whereas those who are half-filled with earthly wisdom make a lot of noise as they blow their own trumpets and declare their "wisdom." Godly people make far less noise and demonstrate true wisdom through their humble lifestyle and kind actions.

---

18. BDAG, *s.v. eritheia.*

Ungodly wisdom has ungodly roots. It "does not come down from heaven but is earthly, unspiritual, demonic" (3:15). Just as temptation does not come from God but flows from the desires of our own hearts (1:14), so ungodly wisdom arises from human selfishness and ambitions. That is why it can be described as "earthly." It is "unspiritual" because it does not link the life of the Spirit of God within us,[19] and ultimately it is "demonic" because it originates with enemies of God and leads to utter alienation from God.[20]

The evil roots of ungodly wisdom are clear from the fruit it produces: "disorder and every evil practice" (3:16). James earlier used the word translated "disorder" to refer to those who are "unstable" (1:8) and referred to the tongue as a "restless" evil (3:8). James does not want to see instability, restlessness, or disorder among Christians, for this will result in disharmony and "every kind of evil practice."

In one of the fifty-five *Dragon-Wisdom Cards of Ancient China*, "desire" is depicted as a green demon with red ears and orange bands on his arms, squatting on the ground and looking up angrily. He is holding a two-pronged fork in his left hand. This is how the image is interpreted:

> Desire, if not attended to, becomes all consuming. . . . Refusal to listen (note the red ears) to the prompting of your spirit, to let go of whatever it is you are now being asked to let go of, must lead, inevitably, to a powerful negative state which will take a powerful hold over your personality for which no one is responsible but you (see how the demon is sitting in his own puddle!). . . . We may have feelings of being betrayed, feelings of self-destruction, or of self-loathing, despair or suicide (note how he is clawing at himself with his right hand). This demon is determined that his position is the true one. He is refusing to listen to anyone.[21]

Earthly, unspiritual, and demonic desires – especially bitter envy and selfish ambition – bring destruction to both individuals and the community. James does not want his readers to face such distress; he wants them to have the heavenly wisdom that is characterized by humility and good deeds.

---

19. 1 Cor 2:14; Jude 19.
20. The adjective *demonic* has the meaning "demon-like," that is, doing things similar to things demons would do (Hort, *The Epistle of St. James*, 84; Davids, *The Epistle of James*, 153; Martin, *James*, 132).
21. Mark Kumara, *The Dragon-Wisdom Cards of Ancient China: Commentaries on The Tao: A Guide to Inner Truth* (Victoria, BC: Trafford Publishing, 2009), 9–10.

3:17 Characteristics of True Wisdom

Earlier James said that "every good and perfect gift comes from above" (1:17). The same is true of the gift of wisdom "that comes from heaven" (3:17a).[22] Godly wisdom originates with God.

In the previous section, James gave two attributes of heavenly wisdom: humility and good deeds (3:13); now he lists seven more attributes. James may have deliberately chosen to mention seven because in Jewish thought the number seven represented completion, perfection, maturity, and perfect wisdom. We see this in the book of Proverbs, where it is said that "Wisdom has built her house; she has set up its seven pillars" (Prov 9:1).[23] The seven characteristics of heavenly wisdom that James lists are that it is pure, peace-loving, considerate, submissive, full of mercy and good fruit, impartial, and sincere.

Wisdom is pure (3:17).[24] Louw-Nida, a Greek lexicon, suggests that this word refers "to being without moral defect or blemish and hence pure." Scientists say that the water flowing from the Himalayas is pure and rich in minerals because it comes from the highest location, where there is almost no pollution. Similarly, wisdom that comes from heaven and God (who is holy and without sin or pollution) is clear of all impurities; it is without moral defects or blemish. Those who manifest such wisdom are similarly pure in their moral character and their wholehearted devotion to Christ (1:27; 2 Cor 11:2).[25]

Wisdom is peace-loving. This word translated "peace-loving" refers to "freedom from anxiety and inner turmoil" (Louw-Nida). Another dictionary defines it as meaning "peaceful" (TDNT). This characteristic of heavenly wisdom manifests itself in believers' own peaceful disposition in times of trials and stress as well as in how they relate to each other. Instead of quickly becoming angry (1:19–20), they will seek to live in harmony with others and to promote peace in the community (see Rom 12:16).

Wisdom is considerate. Those with heavenly wisdom seek to understand the other's point of view. They are gentle, like benevolent leaders who are merciful

---

22. Other Jewish authors write that wisdom is stored in heavenly vaults (Sir 24:5, 8–12).
23. Bauckham, *James*, 177–178. The apocryphal *Wisdom of Solomon* refers to a series of twenty-one epithets used to describe wisdom, which signifies triple perfection (7:22–24). It also gives seven historical illustrations of the saving power of wisdom (Wis 10:1–11:4).
24. This is perhaps an overarching quality of heavenly wisdom since James separates it from the rest of the list with the word "first."
25. In the OT, *pure* referred to cultic objects, prayer, and divine words (Prov 15:26; 19:13; 2 Macc 13.8), but in the NT it refers to moral character and devotion to Christ.

and gracious and bestow honor and blessings, rather than being harsh, un-yielding, quarrelsome and violent (1 Tim 3:3). The Lord Jesus exemplified what it means to be considerate.

Wisdom is submissive. This "submissive" does not mean that wise people do whatever they are told and are subservient. What it means is that people with godly wisdom are open to reason and willing to listen to their opponents. They do not cling to their own opinions. Submissive people are not stubborn individualists, but pay attention to the collective wisdom of a law-abiding community.[26]

Wisdom is full of mercy and good fruit. Although it may seem as if two characteristics are being described here, the Greek structure (two adjectives and two nouns combined by an "and") signals that James is speaking of one mul-tifaceted characteristic. We could put it this way: leaders with godly wisdom overflow with mercy that shows in their actions. "Mercy" here is not used in the sense of "forgiveness" but refers to taking care of and providing for those in need (as in Heb 4:16). James has already referred to this quality in 2:14–17, where he spoke of meeting the material and physical needs of the needy.

Wisdom is impartial. Leaders with godly wisdom do not show favoritism, but are impartial. Unlike those who offered preferential seating to the rich (2:9), leaders with godly wisdom treat everyone with equal honor and respect. They are not susceptible to bribery when making decisions (Exod 23:8; 1 Sam 12:3).

Wisdom is sincere. The Greek word translated as "sincere" means genuine, not hypocritical. Those who are wise, impartial, and willing to be persuaded by clear arguments can be trusted to stick with their decisions once they have considered a case. They are not the sort of people who are constantly changing their minds. Their "yes" means "yes" and their "no" means "no" (Matt 5:37; 2 Cor 1:17–20; Jas 5:12). Thus it is safe to rely on their decisions.

Whereas worldly wisdom (characterized by bitter envy and selfish ambition) will destroy the unity of a congregation, heavenly wisdom (which is pure, peace-loving, considerate, submissive, full of mercy and good fruit, impartial, and sincere) will build their unity and love for one another. So James wants his readers, especially those who are teachers, to have godly wisdom. If they lack it, they should "ask God, who gives generously to all without finding fault" (1:5).

---

26. *Exegetical Dictionary of the New Testament*, 2.81.

3:18 Summary

James is writing to a church that is experiencing problems in terms of the relationship between the rich and the poor, and where many seem to be vying to be teachers or leaders. He advises them to be careful in what they say and do and to seek godly wisdom. Then, as he closes this section, he returns to one of the attributes of heavenly wisdom, saying, "Peacemakers who sow in peace reap a harvest of righteousness" (3:18). Those who are at peace with themselves and committed to peace within the congregation will sow the seed of peace and reap a good harvest. In other words, if teachers work toward bringing peace, their work will be blessed.

Those of us who are committed to bringing peace in our communities should begin by sowing seeds of peace. Eventually, these seeds will grow and yield the fruit of righteousness. This good fruit contrasts with the fruit of "evil desire" – which is death (1:14–15). The idea of a harvest of righteousness springing from sowing peace reminds us of Jesus's blessing in the Sermon on the Mount: "Blessed are the peacemakers, for they will be called children of God" (Matt 5:9). Human anger does not produce the righteousness that God desires (1:20), only divine wisdom can do this.

If the church is to be known as a place of blessing rather than a place of strife, all of us, whether leaders or not, must be people who think before we speak and who sow seeds of peace, inspired by the wisdom that comes from above. Then we will be a force for peace in our wider communities too.

JAMES 4:1–5:20

SPIRITUAL MATURITY IN A COMMUNITY

In chapter 3, James dealt with maturity in speech and wisdom. He stressed the importance of controlling the tongue (3:3–12) and urged his readers to be "peacemakers who sow in peace" and so "reap a harvest of righteousness" (3:18). Keenly aware of the problems caused by a "wisdom" that is "earthly, unspiritual, demonic" (3:15), he now addresses the troubling question of disorder and conflicts within the community.

4:1–10 RESOLVING CONFLICT WITHIN THE COMMUNITY

In this next section, James explains that conflict within the community arises out of greed and envy (4:1–3), that the root cause for this is friendship with the world (4:4–5), and that living humbly before God is the cure (4:6–10).

4:1–3 The Problem: Fighting with Each Other

James begins with a rhetorical question: "What causes fights and quarrels among you?"[1] He then answers his own question: "Don't they come from your desires that battle within you?" (4:1). He is saying that fights and quarrels arise not because of what other people (either inside or outside the community) are doing, nor because believers disagree about particular issues. These are only the secondary causes of the problem. The true causes lie within our own hearts and involve the desires that lurk there. This is alarming! James is saying that often we ourselves, and our internal battles, are the true cause of conflicts within our churches.

Earlier, James made a similar point about desires: "Each person is tempted when they are dragged away by their own evil desire and enticed" (1:14). The Greek word for "desire" (*epithumia*) in 1:14 is neutral and can refer to both good and bad desires. But the word translated "desire" in 4:1 is *hēdonē*, which has negative connotations. It was used to refer to indulgence and unrestrained desire (Luke 8:14; Titus 3:3; 2 Pet 2:13). It is from this Greek word that we get the English word, "hedonism," which refers to being self-indulgent or

---

1. These two sections contain several rhetorical questions (3:13; 4:1, 4, 5). For a study of these, see Luke Timothy Johnson, "James 3:13–4:10 and the *Topos περι φθονου*," *NT* 25, no. 4 (1983): 333. Note that James often uses a question and answer strategy in this epistle (2:4, 5, 6, 7, 14, 15, 16, 20, 21, 25; 3:11, 12, 13; 4:1, 4, 5, 12, 14; 5:6).

pleasure-seeking. Hedonism or self-indulgence was the cause for many of the fights and quarrels within the community.

Earlier James spoke of the interplay of temptation and desire, saying, "Each person is tempted when they are dragged away by their own evil desire and enticed. Then, after desire has conceived, it gives birth to sin; and sin, when it is full-grown, gives birth to death" (1:14–15). He makes a similar link between desire and death here in his blunt assertion, "You desire but do not have, so you kill" (4:2a). His Jewish readers would have been familiar with how this played out in the lives of Ahab, Jezebel, and Naboth: Ahab and Jezebel desired Naboth's vineyard, and when he wouldn't give it to them, they killed him (1 Kgs 21:1–16). Such things did not only happen in the past. In 2013, jealousy led a 13-year-old girl in Guangxi Zhuang to murder her beautiful and popular childhood friend.[2] In 2018 in India, jealousy over a colleague's promotion led to the murder of two of his family members.[3] Jealousy still leads to death.

Unlike the girl from Guangxi Zhuang or the man from India, most people don't resort to murder when they don't get what they want. But they do start quarreling and fighting, as James points out: "You covet but you cannot get what you want, so you quarrel and fight" (4:2b). Covetousness begins with wanting something, but quickly moves to envying what others have. As envy ferments in our hearts it produces anger, which explodes in quarrels and fighting.

Misdirected anger can be avoided if, instead of envying others, Christians bring their needs to God. As James puts it, "you do not have because you do not ask God" (4:2c). God provides all that they need. They can ask God who gives "generously to all without finding fault" for wisdom (1:5), and they can ask him for the other things they long for too.

But what if someone was to argue, "I asked God for something and he didn't give me what I wanted"? James's response is, "When you ask, you do not receive, because you ask with wrong motives, that you may spend what you get on your pleasures (*hēdonē*)" (4:3). God does not want Christians to squander his gifts; when he gives wealth and possessions, he wants us to use them for the benefit of others and not simply for our own enjoyment.

James's warning is one we need to heed today, for many preach a prosperity gospel, promising that God will make us rich and healthy and give us anything

---

2. http://www.chinadaily.com.cn/china/2013-05/07/content_16483323.htm.
3. https://www.deccanchronicle.com/nation/current-affairs/260418/odisha-parcel-bomb-case-lecturer-plotted-attack-out-of-jealousy-sa.html.

we desire. But God does not grant selfish requests. He knows that there is no true or lasting satisfaction in a life devoted solely to our own happiness.

It is not only material things that we covet. Sometime we covet someone else's power or reputation. We want to have the biggest church, or we want to become famous as teachers or preachers. That type of desire may have been behind James's warning against wanting to become a teacher (3:1). Today we see churches divided as leaders wrangle for power. Some start new churches so that they can be in charge. This, too, is a form of hedonism, even though disguised with a cloak of piety and prayer.

John Piper has this to say about the relationship between prayer (asking God for what we need) and desire:

> The central definition of prayer in the Westminster Catechism is "an offering up of our desires unto God." Therefore prayer is the revealer of the heart. What a person prays for shows the spiritual condition of his heart. If we do not pray for spiritual things (like the glory of Christ, and the hallowing of God's name, and the salvation of sinners, and the holiness of our hearts, and the advance of the gospel, and contrition for sin, and the fullness of the Spirit, and the coming of the kingdom, and the joy of knowing Christ), then probably it is because we do not desire these things. Which is a devastating indictment of our hearts.[4]

James would agree. What we should desire is the extension of God's kingdom not the growth of our own bank balances. We who humble ourselves before God and pray for his will, his desires, his kingdom, and his holiness will find that God gives us far more than we ask for. As the Lord said, "Seek first his kingdom and his righteousness, and all these things will be given to you as well" (Matt 6:33).

4:4–5 The Reason: Friendship with the World

Advertisers know how to arouse our desires. The world presents the great deception that pleasures and desires are "needs." Parents must frequently confront this reality. When a teenager says, "I need a motorbike. I can't take the bus to college," is this really a need for transport or just a desire to keep up with "cool" friends?

James was writing to a church where people's desires were running rampant and they were coveting what others had. So James sets out to shock them by

---

4. John Piper, *When I Don't Desire God: How to Fight for Joy* (Wheaton: Crossway, 2013), 139.

addressing them as "You adulterous people" (4:4a). Up to this point in the letter, he has been calling them his beloved brothers and sisters. Why this sudden change?

James is speaking like one of the OT prophets. Ezekiel, for example, wrote, "Then in the nations where they have been carried captive, those who escape will remember me – how I have been grieved by their *adulterous* hearts, which have turned away from me, and by their eyes, which have lusted after their idols. They will loathe themselves for the evil they have done and for all their detestable practices" (Ezek 6:9, italics added). The prophets denounced unfaithfulness to God, his covenant, and his law, using terms like "adulterous" and "unfaithful" (Jer 3:6–10; Ezek 16:23–26; Hos 3:1; 9:1). The prophet Hosea's marriage to an unfaithful wife was a vivid illustration of spiritual adultery (Hos 1:1; 2:2).

James's reference to adultery is intended to shock his readers into realizing that by craving the things that the world wants and values they are being unfaithful to God, so that they, too, are an adulterous generation that has forsaken God and his law. James rebukes them: "Don't you know that friendship with the world means enmity against God? Therefore, anyone who chooses to be a friend of the world becomes an enemy of God" (4:4b). He is warning them that they are as bad as their ancestors who turned their backs on God and worshiped idols! By their infatuation with things that have nothing to do with God, they become enemies of God.

Earlier James spoke about the faithfulness of Abraham who was "called God's friend" (2:23). The people he is writing to are choosing to be friends with the world. But it is impossible to be both a friend of the world and a friend of God. To put it in modern terms, it would be like trying to be both a vegan and a meat-eater at the same time – it cannot be done, for they are polar opposites. Jesus made the same point using a master–servant image: "No one can serve two masters. Either you will hate the one and love the other, or you will be devoted to the one and despise the other. You cannot serve both God and money" (Matt 6:24).

In the ancient world, people were often dependent on the goodwill of wealthy patrons for employment and other privileges. So James's warning against seeking the wrong friendship may also have been intended to warn people against valuing what a human patron could do for them more than what God could do for them. We should not "sell out" to the world to get what we want. We have only one true "patron" and benefactor, namely God himself. Why would we want to exchange the friendship of God for the friendship of the world?

God yearns for fellowship with his children. James writes, "Do you think Scripture says without reason that he jealously longs for the spirit he has caused to dwell in us?" (4:5). Some scholars suggest that James is alluding to Genesis 2:7: "Then the Lord God formed a man from the dust of the ground and breathed into his nostrils the breath of life, and the man became a living being." The word translated "breath" can also be translated "spirit" – God was breathing his spirit into human beings. Having done that, he longs to have fellowship with people, with whom he has shared himself.[5] God's longing for fellowship with his children should drive them to long for fellowship with him, like the psalmist, who cried, "As the deer pants for streams of water, so my soul pants for you, my God" (Ps 42:1). Isaiah expressed a similar sentiment: "My soul yearns for you in the night; in the morning my spirit longs for you" (Isa 26:9).

James's teachings have great relevance for Christians in Asia. We, too, have cultures where the poor depend on the wealthy for jobs, shelter, and basic sustenance, creating patron-client cultures. In such circumstances, we can be tempted to trust the ungodly wealthy for our lives, make friends with them, and collaborate in their sins in order to survive. James's instructions are clear: Don't cultivate friendships with the world; instead, nurture your friendship with God. He longs for our friendship, and he will provide everything we need.

When we are tempted to trust human benefactors who want us to do wrong, we need to have the courage to walk away, trusting God to provide for our needs. This may be difficult when our stomachs are grumbling with hunger pangs, but God is able to deliver us. Our love and longing for him should steer us away from wrongful friendship with the world.

Such a life of trust will come only when we learn to humble ourselves before God and not act arrogantly as if we can sustain ourselves. That is why James now moves on to explain the importance of living humbly before God

---

5. The interpretation of James 4:5 is complex. Is the "spirit" a reference to the Holy Spirit or the human spirit? If it is the latter, is the "spirit" the subject of the verb "to yearn" or its predicate? If the subject, is it a statement or a question? If it is a reference to the Holy Spirit, does it mean, "The Holy Spirit jealously yearns for human love" or "The Holy Spirit in us expresses a longing against human jealousy"? For a detailed study of the various options, see Richard J. Bauckham, "The Spirit of God in Us Loathes Envy (James 4:5)," in *The Holy Spirit and Christian Origin: Essays in Honor of James D. G. Dunn*, eds. G. N. Stanton, B. W. Longenecker and S. C. Barton (Grand Rapids: Eerdmans, 2004), 270–281.

(4:6–10). Thereafter, he will give examples of what pride, the opposite of humility, looks like in daily life (4:11–5:6).

4:6–10 The Solution: Living Humbly Before God

God wants Christians to turn away from friendship with the world and enjoy fellowship with him. Yet, he knows that they are weak, and so he does not immediately punish them when they turn away from him. Instead, "he gives us more grace" (4:6a) – the grace we need to live in fellowship with him. James has already talked of this when he said, "If any of you lacks wisdom, you should ask God, who gives generously to all without finding fault, and it will be given to you" (1:5) and "Every good and perfect gift is from above, coming down from the Father of the heavenly lights" (1:17). All one needs to do to enjoy these blessings is to have the humility to ask for them. When James says, "God opposes the proud but shows favor to the humble" (4:6b), he is quoting Proverbs 3:34: "He [God] mocks proud mockers but shows favor to the humble and oppressed (see also Isa 38:15; Mic 6:8).[6]

James commends humility as the key to living in friendship with God. But what does humility look like? Sounding very like one of the OT prophets who called Israel to repentance (see Hos 14:1–3), James lists eleven actions his readers need to take. He arranges these in a group bookended by the first command ("submit yourselves to God") and the last one ("humble yourselves before the Lord"). The submission required in the first command is absolute surrender, affirming that God alone deserves total loyalty, and the humility required by the last command involves acknowledging that we are utterly dependent on him.

The first command, "Submit yourselves, then, to God" (4:7a), is followed by two commands structured as action and result: "Resist the devil, and he will flee from you. Come near to God and he will come near to you" (4:7b; 4:8a).

Earlier James spoke of envy, selfish ambition, boasting, and denying the truth of God as being worldly wisdom, unspiritual, and demonic (3:14–15). Now, he openly tells the believers to "resist the devil" (4:7b), who is the representative of evil (see Job 1:6–12; 2:1–7) and actively tempts believers to act

---

6. Johnson notes that there are a number of points of contact between Proverbs 3 and James 3:13–4:10: the wisdom of God established the foundation of reality (Prov 3:19); one who follows wisdom will have grace (Prov 3:22); wisdom means walking in the way of peace (Prov 3:23); do not withhold from doing good or tell someone who is in need to come back later (Prov 3:27–28; compare Jas 2:15–16); do not envy the unjust (Prov 3:31), for their way is an abomination to the Lord (Prov 3:32); the wicked will be cursed by God while the righteous will have blessing (Prov 3:22, 35; see also Jas 3:9). Johnson, *The Letter of James*, 385.

in ways that will not please God.[7] As the Apostle Peter warned, he is an enemy who "prowls around like a roaring lion looking for someone to devour" (1 Pet 5:8). Both Peter and James offer the same advice to believers: They must not give up and run away when this "lion" approaches; instead they must "resist him, standing firm in the faith" (1 Pet 5:9). The verb "resist" describes how soldiers respond to an attack. They have no need to fear this enemy; when he is resisted, he turns and runs! He has no power over those who chose to submit to God.

As they resist the devil, believers are to "come near to God" (4:8a), possibly to draw strength from him. They are to approach the presence of God as priests and worshipers did in the OT. While the devil flees, God will draw near and give them more of the power needed to resist the devil. James's words reflect the words of the prophet Zechariah: "This is what the Lord Almighty says: 'Return to me,' declares the Lord Almighty, 'and I will return to you'" (Zech 1:3).

James then gives two more commands that exhort his readers to action. To underscore the importance of what he is saying, he uses language that indicates why the actions are needed, calling his readers "sinners" and "double-minded" (4:8b). True, they have been redeemed from their sins by the blood of Christ, but they are still committing sins of which they need to repent.

The call to "wash your hands" is similar to the call of the OT prophets. Isaiah, for example, wrote, "Your hands are full of blood! Wash and make yourselves clean. Take your evil deeds out of my sight; stop doing wrong" (Isa 1:15–16). Just like OT worshipers, the people James is writing to cleanse or purify themselves before drawing near to God (Job 22:30; Pss 26:6; 34:3–6). But James is not referring to any physical cleansing ritual but to the repentance that cleanses hearts (see Gen 3:22; 4:11; Exod 3:20; Deut 2:7; Ps 90:17).

James's next command parallels the previous one: "Purify your hearts, you double-minded." James sees "sinners" as equivalent to being double-minded. Someone who is wavering in their loyalty to God has been polluted by the world (1:8, 27). They need to cleanse their hearts and return to God. Isaiah continued: "Learn to do right; seek justice. Defend the oppressed. Take up the cause of the fatherless; plead the case of the widow" (Isa 1:16–17). When

---

7. In Jewish tradition, the devil is also referred to as the Prince of Darkness, the Spirit of Error, and Beliar (or Belial); see K. van der Toorn, B. Becking and P. W. van der Horst, eds., *Dictionary of Demons and Deities in the Bible*, 2nd ed. (Leiden: Brill, 1999). In the NT, the names "Satan" and "the devil" are used interchangeably (see Matt 4:1–11; 12:26; 16:23; 25:41; Acts 5:3; 26:18; Rom 16:20; Eph 4:27; 6:11; 1 Tim 3:7; 1 Pet 5:8–9).

believers purify their hearts – by returning to God and by submitting to him – they will do what justice requires: defend the oppressed and protect the widows and the orphans. James earlier mentioned these as examples of "pure religion": "Religion that God our Father accepts as pure and faultless is this: to look after orphans and widows in their distress and to keep oneself from being polluted by the world" (1:27).

Finally, James gives a set of five simple commands: "Grieve, mourn and wail. Change your laughter to mourning and your joy to gloom" (4:9). In the Bible, all these actions are associated with repentance. The prophet Joel, for example, writes: "'Even now,' declares the LORD, 'return to me with all your heart, with *fasting and weeping and mourning*'" (Joel 2:12; italics added; see also Isa 15:2; Jer 4:13; Hos 10:5). When Jonah's preaching convinced the people of Nineveh of their impending peril, "A fast was proclaimed, and all of them, from the greatest to the least, put on sackcloth . . . When Jonah's warning reached the king of Nineveh, he rose from his throne, took off his royal robes, covered himself with sackcloth and sat down in the dust" (Jonah 3:5–6). True repentance is often embarrassing, shameful, and painful. It requires us to look at reality differently, evaluating our spiritual condition from the perspective of God and recognizing our weakness and depravity. James, like his prophetic predecessors, longs to see this type of repentance among those who have rebelled against God.

When believers manifest true repentance, they will enjoy God's blessing. That is why Paul can say that "Godly sorrow brings repentance that leads to salvation and leaves no regret" (2 Cor 7:10). The repentant obey James's eleventh command: "Humble yourselves before the Lord, and he will lift you up" (4:10). To humble oneself means "to recognize our own spiritual poverty, to acknowledge consequently our desperate need of God's help, and to submit to his commanding will for our lives."[8]

James wants his readers to repent of the selfish desires that had infected their church and resulted in fights and quarrels (4:1). When they did not get what they wanted, they did not ask God for it but, instead, tried to get it in ungodly ways. Whatever they wanted – material possessions or status in the church or community – they were trying to get it in the wrong way. So James concludes this section by reminding them that if they submit to God and

---

8. Moo, *The Letter of James*, 196.

humble themselves to his will, he will provide what they need and lift them up. But he will do this in his own time and in his own way.[9]

Instead of trusting in our own abilities or seeking our own ways to gain material blessings or other honors, we, too, must ask God for what we want, submit to him, and draw near to him. At the right time, he will provide what we need, and do so generously. He alone knows what we need (which we often confuse with what we want).

4:11–5:6 PRIDE IN DAILY LIFE

In the previous section, James shocked his readers by calling them, "adulterous," "sinners," and "double-minded." But now he reverts to the more loving language he used in the rest of his letter and addresses them as his "brothers and sisters" as he gives examples of the ways that pride, the opposite of humility, manifests itself in their daily lives.

4:11–12 Pride and Slander

James's call to humility is followed immediately by a simple command: "Do not slander one another" (4:11a). To slander someone is to intentionally spread distorted information about them that discredits them, tarnishes their reputation, and even "demonizes" them. Such behavior is explicitly prohibited in the Ten Commandments (Exod 20:16) and in the book of Leviticus: "Do not go about spreading slander among your people. Do not do anything that endangers your neighbor's life, I am the LORD" (Lev 19:16). Slander is also condemned in the NT (Rom 1:30; 2 Cor 12:20; 1 Pet 2:1). Slander often arises from the envy and ambition that James has already condemned (3:14; 4:2) and is sometimes equivalent to murder since it can destroy someone.

James recognizes that slander is rooted in pride: "Anyone who speaks against a brother or sister or judges them speaks against the law and judges it. When you judge the law, you are not keeping it, but sitting in judgment on it" (4:11). Slanderers think they know better than God and his revealed law! They judge others by the law while they themselves disobey the law. Paul also pointed out the error of such an action: "You, therefore, have no excuse, you who pass judgment on someone else, for at whatever point you judge another,

---

9. This same point is made in the second half of Proverbs 3:34, which takes us back to the point made by James in 4:6–7. This eleventh command concludes the entire section from James 4:1. It forms an *inclusio* with the command to "submit yourselves to God" in James 4:7a and reflects the second part of the quotation of Proverbs 3:34 in James 4:5.

you are condemning yourself, because you who pass judgment do the same things" (Rom 2:1). The Lord Jesus, too, warned against such a dangerous stance: "In the same way you judge others, you will be judged, and with the measure you use, it will be measured to you" (Matt 7:2). When believers take it upon themselves to be the judge of other people by using the law, they must be prepared to face the same law's judgment upon themselves. That's because ultimately there is one impartial judge: "There is only one Lawgiver and Judge, the one who is able to save and destroy" (4:12a).

Just as there is only one Lord, so there is only one lawgiver, judge, savior, and executioner – God. How dare James's audience presume to write new laws for others or to judge others based upon their own laws or even by God's law which they themselves don't obey? Judgment is God's prerogative.

James concludes: "But you – who are you to judge your neighbor?" (4:12b). Earlier he had spoken of the royal law: "Love your neighbor as yourself" (2:8); the royal law is not: "Judge your neighbor by yourself." To judge others by the law while not obeying the law amounts to slandering and gossiping. Christians should leave judgment to God, whose judgment is always fair and truthful.

Neither James nor the Lord Jesus Christ is saying that there is no place for discernment and judgment and rejecting what is wrong. In this very letter, James clearly condemns certain behaviors. So this command does not mean that the church cannot judge between right and wrong. The Scriptures clearly teach that we should discern between good and bad (1 Cor 2:14; 10:15; 11:13; Phil 1:10). They also command us to evaluate our own actions by God's standards (1 Cor 6:2, 4; Heb 4:12). What James is condemning here is judging someone *falsely*, that is, by our own standards or laws that are tainted by wrong motives, or hypocritically judging others while we ourselves do the same things.

When tempted to make judgments based on human wisdom and standards, we do well to remember that human opinions are not fixed, but fluid and fluctuating. Fifty years ago, many Christians condemned those who watched movies; now Christians watch movies on their television screens. Fifty years ago, some Christians condemned songs accompanied by drums as demonic; now they call them worship songs. It is quite likely that our opinions on "spiritual discipline" (based on our own standards) will also not stand the test of time. Our standards and rules are often based on imperfect information and our own biases, and sometimes, on our desire to exalt our preferred form of spirituality – is that not a type of selfish ambition?

God's judgment is impartial, fair, and unchanging. At the right time he will judge people by his own laws, either saving them or punishing them. We are to leave judgment in his capable hands.

4:13–16 Pride and Plans

James has warned prideful people, "God opposes the proud but shows favor to the humble" (4:6) and exhorted his readers, "Humble yourselves before the Lord, and he will lift you up" (4:10). Now he addresses one specific expression of pride: autonomy in decision-making (4:13–16).

James imagines an entrepreneur, trader, or merchant making plans: "Today or tomorrow we will go to this or that city, spend a year there, carry on business and make money" (4:13).[10] This person is laying out his time schedule and has no doubt carefully chosen a city with many business opportunities. The goal is to make a profit and increase wealth. James does not criticize planning; what he does object to is anyone assuming that they are in control of what is going to happen and that their plans will all fall neatly into place. His words echo the warning in the book of Proverbs: "Do not boast about tomorrow, for you do not know what a day may bring" (Prov 27:1). The boastful autonomy of this merchant in ignoring the sovereignty of God resembles the thinking of the rich man in the Lord Jesus's parable. The rich man said to himself, "You have plenty of grain laid up for many years. Take life easy; eat, drink and be merry." But in the parable, God said to him, "You fool! This very night your life will be demanded from you. Then who will get what you have prepared for yourself?" (Luke 12:16–20).

James warns confident planners, "Why, you do not even know what will happen tomorrow. What is your life? You are a mist that appears for a little while and then vanishes" (4:14).[11] He made a similar point at the start of his letter when he said, "The rich . . . will pass away like a wild flower. For the sun rises with scorching heat and withers the plant . . . In the same way, the rich will fade away even while they go about their business" (1:9–10).

James's warning does not apply only to the rich. Since none of us can count on what will happen tomorrow, let alone in the more distant future, we should not be presumptuous in planning our future while leaving God out

---

10. James begins the verse with the words, "Now listen, you who say." This is a literary device to introduce arguments addressing imaginary opponents. For more information on trading activities in first-century Roman Palestine, see Pedrito U. Maynard-Reid, *Poverty and Wealth in James* (Maryknoll: Orbis, 1987), 71–111.

11. In Greek, the participles *appear* and *vanish* have the same root, but they mean exact opposites, like the English pair "appears" and "disappears."

of our plans. A Chinese proverb says that life is short and fleeting as morning dew, changing as unpredictably as a floating cloud. For all of us, life is like the early morning mist that evaporates soon after the sun rises (see also Pss 37:20; 68:2; Hos 13:3). This mist is transient and insubstantial; it has neither permanence nor strength. The same is true of us – we are here on this earth for a brief moment in time.

Since life is uncertain, James wants believers to plan their future in accordance with God's will: "Instead, you ought to say, 'If it is the Lord's will, we will live and do this or that'" (4:15). Every plan and decision should be made in humble dependence on God and in submission to his sovereignty. That is the measure of true humility.

Sometimes people use the phrase "God willing" casually, almost as a punctuation mark. That is not what James expects of us. Rather, he wants to shatter any illusions of autonomy and help us recognize God's sovereignty over all our plans. We plan but do so knowing that God is in control of our future and submitting ourselves to his will. The Lord Jesus's prayer at Gethsemane illustrates this attitude: "My Father, if it is possible, may this cup be taken from me. Yet not as I will, but as you will" (Matt 26:39). Jesus desired that the cup of death be taken from him. But he submitted his desires to God's will. True humility is to plan our future saying to ourselves, "I want God's will to be done."

James concludes this section by confronting his readers: "As it is, you boast in your arrogant schemes. All such boasting is evil" (4:16). The schemes are arrogant because the planners are arrogant. They are "practical atheists" – while not actually denying that God exists, they live as if he does not exist and devote their energy to their own success. Such a shortsighted perspective is evil.

We, too, are practical atheists if we live as if God were only interested in our spiritual life and unconcerned with how we live and the circumstances of our lives. God takes a personal interest in every aspect of our earthly lives. That is why Jesus taught his disciples to pray, "Your kingdom come, your will be done, on earth as it is in heaven" (Matt 6:10).

4:17 Pride and Disobedience

So far, James has addressed how pride may manifest itself in slander (4:11–12) or arrogant autonomy which makes plans without reference to God (4:13–16). Now he turns his attention to those who know the instructions of the Scriptures but do nothing about them. James warns, "If anyone, then, knows the good they ought to do and doesn't do it, it is sin for them" (4:17).

Earlier, James wrote that those who know the law but don't obey it are "deceived" (1:22). He illustrated their folly by saying, "Anyone who listens to the word but does not do what it says is like someone who looks at his face in a mirror and, after looking at himself, goes away and immediately forgets what he looks like" (1:23–24). Now he goes further, insisting that failure to follow through with prompt obedience is sin.

The people James has been rebuking for their uncontrolled desires (1:15), favoritism (2:9), fighting (4:1), and arrogance (4:16) took pride in knowing the OT Scriptures, yet they were failing to obey them. Are we, in Asia, any less guilty? We take pride in our knowledge of the Scriptures, but we frequently fail to obey it. We start quarrels and fights because we are jealous of what others have, and we refuse to ask, or trust, God to provide what we need. We slander others for not keeping God's law while we ourselves do not keep his word. We favor the wealthy, the educated, or the influential, but despise the needy, the oppressed, the marginalized. We plan our future – making five-year or ten-year plans – without reference to God's will and his purpose for our lives. In all these instances, we fail to do what we *know* is right – and so, we sin. The Scriptures are not given to us merely to be read, but to be faithfully and promptly obeyed.

5:1–6 Pride and Self-indulgence

James begins 5:1 with the words, "Now listen," the same words he used in 4:13, suggesting that in this paragraph he is still talking about wrong attitudes in Christians' daily lives. In 4:13, he was addressing people who were planning to get wealthy through travel and trade; now he talks to those who are already wealthy, addressing them as "you rich people." This is the third time James has talked about the rich in this letter (see also 1:10–11; 2:5–6), suggesting that there were several wealthy people in the churches he was addressing. Even if this was not the case, there were certainly plenty of rich people in the surrounding community whose lifestyles might look attractive to some. So James speaks to warn the rich, to discourage those who are tempted to imitate them, and to encourage poor Christians who were being exploited by the rich.

God is not opposed to Christians making plans or to rich people. What he is opposed to are plans that ignore him (4:13–16) and rich people who are arrogant in their disregard for God and his law. God blessed people like Abraham, Job, David, and Solomon with wealth, and James has already praised Abraham

(2:21–23) and will soon praise Job (5:11).[12] But God opposes the self-indulgent rich who exploit those who work for them and gain wealth illicitly.

James sounds a frightening warning to such people: "Now listen, you rich people, weep and wail because of the misery that is coming on you" (5:1; see also 4:9). The language James uses – "listen," "weep," and "wail"[13] – is similar to that of the OT prophets when they called the Israelites to repentance (Isa 15:2; Jer 4:13; Hos 10:5; Joel 2:12).[14] The unjust rich need to repent; if they do not, misery will soon come upon them.

James is not necessarily referring to the punishment that awaits the arrogant rich on the day of judgment (5:1).[15] He may be thinking of more immediate miseries that await them: "Your wealth has rotted, and moths have eaten your clothes. Your gold and silver are corroded" (5:2–3a). Wealth often slips away from the rich, as vividly demonstrated in the stories of those who have won millions in lotteries and yet, end up destitute.[16]

James also reminds his readers of the impermanence of riches. The fancy clothes people wear to signal their status soon become worn and moth-eaten. Even metals like silver and gold lose their shine. James is echoing the Lord's teaching: "Do not store up for yourselves treasures on earth, where moths and vermin destroy, and where thieves break in and steal. But store up for yourselves treasures in heaven, where moths and vermin do not destroy, and where thieves do not break in and steal" (Matt 6:19–20). The natural processes that destroy material wealth serve to illustrate an important truth: the rich should never assume that wealth guarantees a good life. After all, life itself is only "a mist that appears for a little while and then vanishes" (4:14; see also Luke

---

12. Briel makes a similar observation. Steven C. Briel, "18th Sunday after Trinity: James 5:1–11," *Concordia Theological Quarterly* 46, no. 1 (1982): 75.

13. The term for "wail" *ololyzō* (different to "cry" in Jas 4:9) is onomatopoeic – that is, the vocalization imitates the sound of the act being described (as with the *hiss* of a cobra or the *buzzing* of a bee).

14. James 5:1–6 reflects the style of the prophetic speech in the OT that included four basic components: (1) an introductory word with an appeal for attention (2 Kgs 1:3; Amos 7:16; 2 Kgs 20:16; Jer 28:15; Isa 7:13; Jas 5:1a), (2) the "indication of the situation" or accusation (Jas 5:4–6), (3) the "prediction of disaster" or "announcement of judgment" (2 Sam 12:11; 1 Kgs 11:31; 13:2; 20:36; Jer 20:3; 29:21; Jas 5:4), and (4) the "concluding characterization" (Jas 5:4, 6b). For a detailed study, see W. E. March, "Prophecy," in *Old Testament Form Criticism*, ed. J. H. Hayes (San Antonio: Trinity University Press, 1974), 159–160 and C. Westermann, *Basic Forms of Prophetic Speech*, trans. H. C. White (London: Lutterworth, 1967), 142–148.

15. Although that interpretation is possible (Moo, *Letter of James*, 211).

16. See http://www.businessinsider.in/21-lottery-winners-who-blew-it-all/articleshow/50475628.cms.

12:16–20). When life disappears, all that the rich have accumulated (legally or illegally) will be left behind for others to enjoy.

Wealth and possessions also testify against their owners: "Their corrosion will testify against you" (5:3b). The moth-eaten garments and the rusted metal will be evidence that these things were hoarded rather than being used as God intended. The Scriptures often talk about inanimate objects testifying against people. When Cain murdered Abel, God said, "Your brother's blood cries out to me from the ground" (Gen 4:10). When the Pharisees demanded that the Lord Jesus stop people acknowledging him as the coming king, he said, "If they keep quiet, the stones will cry out" (Luke 19:40; see also Hab 2:11). Even wealth will serve as evidence against the rich and "eat your flesh like fire." Rather than making the arrogant rich comfortable, their riches will metaphorically burn them.

Instead of using their wealth to help the poor, they have "hoarded wealth in the last days" (5:3c). Some interpret this as meaning that they were storing up judgment *for* the last days, a reference to future judgment (see Ps 21:9; Isa 30:27; Ezek 15:7; Amos 1:12, 14; 5:6; 7:4). However, the word used is "in," which suggests that James is accusing them of failing to use their wealth wisely *in these last days,* that is, the new era that began with Christ's death and resurrection (see Acts 2:17; Heb 1:2; 2 Pet 3:3). The Lord Jesus himself instructed his followers: "Sell your possessions and give to the poor. Provide purses for yourselves that will not wear out, a treasure in heaven that will never fail, where no thief comes near and no moth destroys" (Luke 12:33). When the rich use their wealth to care for the poor and needy, they are not hoarding wealth in these days, but they are storing indestructible treasure in heaven. Instead of merely accumulating wealth in this world, they are investing it in God's kingdom.

Hoarding wealth was bad enough. But the rich were also gaining wealth illegally: "Look! The wages you failed to pay the workers who mowed your fields are crying out against you. The cries of the harvesters have reached the ears of the Lord Almighty" (5:4). The employers (or landowners) were exploiting the laborers who worked in their fields and withholding the wages of those who harvested the field.[17] The OT explicitly forbids exploitation: "Do not defraud or rob your neighbor. Do not hold back the wages of a hired

---

17. For an account of the political economy in Roman Palestine and how the ruling class took control of the land (the most important resource) and labor through indebtedness, see K. C. Hanson and D. E. Oakman, *Palestine in the Time of Jesus: Social Structures and Social Conflicts* (Minneapolis: Fortress, 1998), 99–129.

worker overnight" (Lev 19:13) and "Do not take advantage of a hired worker who is poor and needy, whether that worker is a fellow Israelite or a foreigner residing in one of your towns. Pay them their wages each day before sunset, because they are poor and are counting on it" (Deut 24:14–15; see also Jer 22:13; Mal 3:5). Yet, the rich were ignoring these commands and were not paying proper wages to the laborers and harvesters.

The situation James describes is also evident in Asia today. In India, for example, generations of families are trapped in bonded labor, forced to work for little or nothing to pay off debts that are constantly growing. No Christian employer should be guilty of exploiting workers in this manner. Nor should Christian householders abuse domestic servants. Instead, Christians should be known for the fairness with which they treat their workers, never withholding their wages or oppressing them, but paying fair wages and providing decent working conditions.

The rich assumed that poor laborers were defenseless, and that no one would hear their cries or challenge the actions of the rich. But the apparently defenseless poor have a defender. God, the ultimate lawgiver and judge, hears their cries: "The cries of the harvesters have reached the ears of the Lord Almighty" (5:4b). The OT also predicted this: "Pay them . . . . Otherwise they may cry to the LORD against you, and you will be guilty of sin" (Deut 24:15). The Lord Almighty himself defends poor laborers against the rich.

The designation "the Lord Almighty" occurs over 245 times in the OT, but only this one time in the NT. It presents God as a powerful king, leading his great army to fight against his enemies, bringing swift judgment on them for their disobedience and disloyalty. Although the rich thought there was no one to defend the poor laborers and harvesters that they were oppressing, they were very much mistaken! God is defending them. James does not state what action the Lord God Almighty will take against the wicked rich, but he assures his readers that God Almighty takes the plight of the poor seriously.

When God judges the rich, he will find them guilty on several counts: "You have lived on earth in luxury and self-indulgence. You have fattened yourselves in the day of slaughter. You have condemned and murdered the innocent one, who was not opposing you" (5:5–6).

First, they "lived on earth in luxury" (5:5a). The Lord Jesus described such a lifestyle: "There was a rich man who was dressed in purple and fine linen and lived in luxury every day" (Luke 16:19). This man wore the best clothes and ate the best food, unlike the poor beggar, Lazarus, who was "covered with sores and longing to eat what fell from the rich man's table" (Luke 16:20b–21).

Similarly, the wicked whom James is describing "have lived on earth in luxury." But they will only enjoy such a life "on earth" – things will be very different in the afterlife, as the rich man in the Lord's parable discovered to his horror (Luke 16:19–31).

Second, they have "lived on earth in . . . self-indulgence" (5:5a). Earlier James explained that temptations are rooted in uncontrolled desires (1:14–15) that lead to quarreling and death (4:1–2). God does not give people just what they want because they want to use it for selfish pleasures (4:3). The unjust rich epitomize such desires. They are interested only in themselves and do not seek the best for others. They fund their luxuries with unpaid wages.

Third, they "have fattened [themselves] in the day of slaughter" (5:5c). James borrowed the phrase "day of slaughter" from the prophet Jeremiah, who said, "Drag them off like sheep to be butchered! Set them apart for the day of slaughter!" (Jer 12:3). Jeremiah criticized those who praised God but didn't live as God's people: "You [Lord God] are always on their lips but far from their hearts" (Jer 12:2). Their words and lifestyles didn't match. Similarly, James accuses the rich of fattening themselves with the wages that belonged to the poor. Whereas the rich thought they were fattening themselves for comfort, luxury, and safety, they were actually fattening themselves to be slaughtered (just as the fattest calves and sheep were slaughtered and sacrificed – 1 Sam 28:24; 2 Sam 6:13; 1 Kgs 1:9; Prov 15:17).

Fourth, they "have condemned . . . the innocent one" (5:6a). Earlier, James spoke about the irony of inappropriately honoring the rich and asked, "Is it not the rich who are exploiting you? Are they not the ones who are dragging you into court? Are they not the ones who are blaspheming the noble name of him to whom you belong?" (2:2–7). The ungodly rich often harm those who have done nothing to them, treating them as if they count for nothing.

Fifth, the unrighteous rich have "murdered the innocent one, who was not opposing" them (5:6b).[18] James uses hyperbole (exaggeration) when he says, "You desire but do not have, so you kill" (4:2a), and he is probably doing the same here.[19] The poor lived a hand-to-mouth existence, like many do today, and if they were not paid, they did not eat (Deut 24:15). When the rich did

---

18. Byron explains that in Jewish writings Cain who killed his brother Abel (Gen 4) was portrayed as an archetype of those who oppressed the poor, even withholding their wages. John Byron, "Living in the Shadow of Cain: Echoes of a Developing Tradition in James 5:1–6," *NovT* 48, no. 3 (2006): 261–274.
19. Since James used an articular singular, "the righteous one," some have proposed that he was talking about the Lord or about his own fate. Mayor, *Epistle of St. James*, 160; M. Dibelius, *A*

not pay their laborers, the laborers and their families starved. Their deaths were rightly blamed on the rich. The Jewish writer Ben Sira said, "The bread of the needy is the life of the poor; whoever deprives them of it is a murderer. To take away a neighbor's living is to commit murder; to deprive an employee of wages is to shed blood" (Sir 34:25–27). This resembles James's teaching in 5:6. So their blood cried out to God for justice, just like the blood of Abel (Gen 4:10). The poor had done nothing to deserve such treatment.[20]

The rich in many cultures behave like this. A poem by Duo Fu, the great poet of the Tang Dynasty, makes this clear. He was a poor man who eventually managed to secure a minor government position, and hurried home to tell the good news to his wife and son. On his way, he passed the emperor's summer palace and saw leftover food thrown in the garden to rot. When he reached home, he learned that his son had died of hunger. He immediately composed a poem to mourn his son and to point out the extreme disparity between the rich and the poor:

> Behind the red doors wine and meat go to waste
> While outside on the road lie the bones of the frozen.[21]

Extreme disparity between rich and poor is still common in Asia. Although poverty has been significantly reduced in the past decades, the rich are getting richer far faster than the poor. Despite the growth in the national GDP, the Gini coefficient that captures inequality per capita expenditure worsened in twelve economies, including the People's Republic of China, India, Indonesia, and Hong Kong.[22]

An Oxfam report says that since 2015 the richest 1 percent have owned more wealth than the rest of the planet. It says that over the next twenty years, 500 people will hand over $2.1 trillion to their heirs – a sum larger than the annual GDP of India, a country with 1.3 billion people. Between 1988 and

---

Commentary on the Epistle of James, trans. M. A. Williams, Hermeneia (Philadelphia: Fortress, 1976), 240 n. 58. But Jewish writings with similar context consider the poor as the righteous people (*Wisdom of Solomon* 2:10–12).
20. For other interpretations of this verse, see L. A. Schökel, "James 5, 2 [*sic*] and 4, 6," *Biblica* 54 (1973): 73–74; Johnson, *The Letter of James*, 305. For a comparison between James and Amos, see William M. Tillman, "Social Justice in the Epistle of James," *Review and Expositor* 108 (2011): 417–427. Hiebert explains that the poor's moral uprightness and just acts would themselves have aroused the hatred among the sinful rich. E. Edmond Hiebert, *James* (Chicago: Moody Press, 1992), 268.
21. https://www.reddit.com/r/ChapoTrapHouse/comments/6pkd4c/behind_the_red_doors_wine_and_meat_go_to_waste/.
22. *Asian Development Outlook 2012*, released by Asian Development Bank, Manila: Philippines, 2012, p. xviii.

2011 the incomes of the poorest 10 percent increased by just $65, while the incomes of the richest 1 percent grew by $11,800 – 182 times as much.[23] These figures are alarming.

In this present world, James's teachings on wealth and riches are pertinent. God gives grace to all, including the poor, and answers prayers that are not motivated by selfish ambitions. He also holds the rich accountable for the use they make of their wealth. If they gain their wealth by exploiting the poor, or selfishly hoard their wealth, they will face God's judgment.[24] God blesses us so that we can be a blessing to those around us.

5:7–20 MATURITY IN DAILY LIFE

After explaining how Christians should avoid the evils of pride, James begins a new section with his usual address to his "brothers and sisters" to whom he is going to give further advice for daily living as Christians. He uses this expression four times in this section of the letter (5:7, 10, 12, 19), signaling that he cares about them in their suffering. He may also be implying that, as part of the same Christian family, he can identify with them for he, too, has had to face injustice.

This section on suffering is linked to the previous verses by the conjunction "therefore" (5:7a, translated "then" in the NIV), which implies that it is the greed of the rich that causes the suffering of the poor.

5:7–11 Responding to Suffering

James began this letter by advising his readers on how to handle trials and sufferings" (1:2) and he returns to that theme at the end of his letter. He begins with a command: "Be patient, then, brothers and sisters, until the Lord's coming" (5:7a). When facing injustice, poverty, cruelty, and exploitation, it is tempting to retaliate with anger and violence. But James urges Christians to be patient until the Lord's coming, implying that the Lord will secure justice for them and fight on their behalf.[25] This, too, is in line with OT teaching: "Do not seek revenge or bear a grudge against anyone among your people, but love your neighbor as yourself. I am the LORD" (Lev 19:18); and "It is mine to avenge; I will repay" (Deut 32:35). Paul quotes the latter passage in his letter

---

23. https://www.theguardian.com/global-development/2017/jan/16/worlds-eight-richest-people-have-same-wealth-as-poorest-50.
24. Moo, *The Letter of James*, 200. For contextualizing James 5:1–6 in a South African context, see Hartin, "'Come Now, You Rich, Weep and Wail . . .' (James 5:1-6)," 57–63.
25. James uses two Greek synonyms for "patience" a total of seven times in these verses.

to the church in Rome (Rom 12:19). Similarly, James asks his readers to be patient until the Lord himself will vindicate his people at the end of the age.[26] He offers three examples of patience, namely farmers, the prophets, and Job.

His first example is drawn from farming: "See how the farmer waits for the land to yield its valuable crop, patiently waiting for the autumn and spring rains" (5:7b). The word "see" invites us to visualize a farmer sitting by a field that has been dug, prepared, and planted.[27] Now there is nothing more the farmer can do except wait for the rain to come so the seeds will sprout and grow into a healthy crop.[28] In Israel, the autumn rain came from mid-October to mid-November and the spring rain came from March to April. Prophets spoke of the regular arrival of these rains as symbolic of God's providential care for his people (Deut 11:14; Jer 5:24; Joel 2:23; Zech 10:1).

The patience of a farmer relying on the Lord (5:7) is in sharp contrast to the arrogance of the merchants (4:13–16) and the oppressive behavior of the rich (5:1–6) who consider themselves self-sufficient. They will reap condemnation and destruction (4:11, 17; 5:5), whereas, the humble farmer will reap blessing (5:8, 11). Living in the light of the coming of the Lord is to live in his presence and acknowledge his sovereignty in our present struggles.

James repeats his point for emphasis: "You too, be patient and stand firm [literally, "strengthen your hearts"] because the Lord's coming is near" (5:8).[29] Earlier James said that the rich were "fattening their hearts for the day of slaughter" (5:5); now he exhorts his readers to "strengthen their hearts" since the Lord's coming is near (5:8). At any moment, the Lord may come and usher in the final fulfillment of kingdom of God. God will help them as they try and strengthen their hearts (Rom 1:11; 1 Thess 3:2, 13; 2 Thess 2:17; 3:3; Heb 13:9; 1 Pet 5:10; 2 Pet 1:12; Rev 3:2).

When oppressed, people tend to respond with anger and frustration. They may start grumbling against one another, ignoring the command to love our neighbors as ourselves, and so create distrust and disorder in the community (3:16). So James writes, "Don't grumble against one another, brothers and sisters, or you will be judged" (5:9a). Here, too, he is reflecting OT teaching:

---

26. The phrase "the Lord's coming" is a technical term for the coming of the Lord Jesus as judge at the final judgment (1 Thess 2:19; 3:13; 4:15; 5:23; 2 Thess 2:1, 8). This event is also referred to as the coming of the Son of Man (Matt 24:3, 27, 37, 39) and the coming of Christ (1 Cor 15:23).
27. The interjection "see" occurs three times in this section (5:7, 9, 11).
28. The present (gnomic) verb emphasizes the regular waiting of a farmer.
29. The verb in the present tense accentuates the reality of the Lord's coming and reflects the Gospels (Matt 3:2; 4:17; 10:7; Mark 1:15; Luke 10:9, 11).

"Do not seek revenge *or bear a grudge* against anyone among your people, but love your neighbor as yourself. I am the LORD" (Lev 19:18; italics added). If those who are oppressed control their emotions and wait for the Lord to avenge them, he will act in justice, in his own time, and the community will not suffer harm because of festering anger.

James reassures his readers, "The Judge is standing at the door!" (5:9b).[30] The oppressed can safely leave judgment to the Lord at his second coming. But these words are also a warning: The Lord God is the righteous judge (4:12), and he will judge the oppressed, too, if they sin in their response to oppression.

James's basic lesson is that the congregations should not be filled with grumbling against fellow believers or harbor thoughts of revenge. He is not saying that Christians cannot denounce social injustice; nor is he advising them never to speak out against oppression. We can say this confidently on the basis of his next example of patience, namely "the prophets who spoke in the name of the Lord" (5:10).[31] James was probably thinking of prophets like Jeremiah, who was beaten and imprisoned (Jer 20:1–2; 26:7–9; 36:24–26); Isaiah, who according to Jewish tradition was eventually martyred by being sawn in two (Heb 11:37); and many others mentioned in the OT and NT (Matt 5:12; 23:34–37; Luke 6:23; 11:49–51; 13:33; 24:25; Acts 7:52; Rom 11:3; 1 Thess 2:15; Heb 11:32–38). Despite facing persecution and accusations that they were spreading rumors and threatening the security of the nation, these prophets patiently continued their ministries, in the course of which they exhorted God's people to defend the rights of the oppressed. Isaiah, for example, called on God's people to "learn to do right; seek justice. Defend the oppressed. Take up the cause of the fatherless; plead the case of the widow" (Isa 1:17). These prophets endured tremendous pressures from the people and tyrannical rulers, but they did not take up arms. They allowed the Lord to fight their battles as they prophesied in his name and denounced injustice. They set an example that James wants his readers to follow so that they, in turn, can become examples to others. We, too, should stand up for the rights of refugees, the homeless, and any who are oppressed, regardless of their gender, age, ethnicity or culture.

---

30. Other NT writers use the imagery of the Lord standing at the door to emphasize his immanence and proximity (Mark 13:29; Rev 3:20). For a study of door imagery in ancient days, see Marianne Sawicki, "Person or Practice? Judging in James and in Paul," in *The Mission of James, Peter, and Paul: Tensions in Early Christianity*, ed. Bruce D. Chilton and Craig Evans (Leiden: Brill, 2005), 393.
31. James also uses OT examples in his references to Abraham and Rahab in 2:21–25.

We can also learn from Jesus's example. He was not someone who grumbled or encouraged violence, but when he was wrongfully slapped he challenged the official who had done it, saying "If I spoke the truth, why did you strike me?" (John 18:23). Paul, too, endured suffering patiently. But when he was wrongfully imprisoned in Philippi and the magistrates wanted to quietly send him away, Paul responded: "'They beat us publicly without a trial, even though we are Roman citizens, and threw us into prison. And now do they want to get rid of us quietly? No! Let them come themselves and escort us out'" (Acts 16:37).

Like the prophets, our Lord, and Paul, we should be willing to speak out for justice while being careful that we do not sin in the process of defending it. And sometimes, our response to oppression should be in the form of action rather than words. For example, South Korean Pastor Lee Jong-rak was horrified that people were abandoning unwanted babies and leaving them to die. So he installed a heated box outside his home where people could leave babies anonymously. He took care of these babies and found them homes.[32]

James adds extra weight to his exhortation to patience in 5:7 when he adds, "As you know, we count as blessed those who have persevered" (5:11a).[33] Here he is reflecting Jesus's words in the Sermon on the Mount: "Blessed are you when people insult you, persecute you and falsely say all kinds of evil against you because of me. Rejoice and be glad, because great is your reward in heaven, for in the same way they persecuted the prophets who were before you" (Matt 5:11–12). Our natural inclination when facing persecution is either to retaliate against the oppressors or to give up. But blessing comes through perseverance. As the African scholar Solomon Andria writes, "Anyone who loves God may have to face suffering, but by the end of it they will know God better, and have a far deeper understanding of his love and mercy."[34]

James now gives a third example of perseverance in the midst of trials and sufferings: "You have heard of Job's perseverance and have seen what the Lord finally brought about" (5:11b). This reference to Job implies that the patience James is speaking of is not just patience in the face of injustice, but also patience in the face of the adversities of life (see 1:2). Job lost his possessions,

---

32. https://www.independent.co.uk/news/world/asia/south-korean-church-leader-who-set-up-drop-box-to-adopt-unwanted-babies-sees-trailer-for-documentary-9110001.html.
33. The phrase "as you know" is "behold" (ιδου) in Greek. This is the third time James uses this expression in this subsection to draw attention to what he is saying.
34. Solomon Andria, "James," in *Africa Bible Commentary*, edited by Tokunboh Adeyemo (Grand Rapids: Zondervan, 2006), 1541.

family, and health. His wife and friends failed him. An apocryphal writing known as the *Testament of Job*, starts with his confession, "I am your father, fully engaged in endurance," and concluded with an exhortation to endure: "Now then, my children, you also must be patient in everything that happens to you. For patience is better than anything."[35] The Bible describes Job's final reward as follows:

> The Lord blessed the latter part of Job's life more than the for-
> mer part. He had fourteen thousand sheep, six thousand cam-
> els, a thousand yoke of oxen and a thousand donkeys. And he
> also had seven sons and three daughters. The first daughter
> he named Jemimah, the second Keziah and the third Keren-
> Happuch. Nowhere in all the land were there found women
> as beautiful as Job's daughters, and their father granted them
> an inheritance along with their brothers. After this, Job lived a
> hundred and forty years; he saw his children and their children
> to the fourth generation. And so Job died, an old man and full
> of years. (Job 42:12–17)

After giving Job as an example, James concludes: "The Lord is full of compassion and mercy" (5:11c).[36] By referring to God's character, James is assuring his readers that God will not remain quiet for long. He will act on behalf of the oppressed. If Christians persevere through sufferings without planning vengeance or constant grumbling, God will take their side and defend them.

This passage in James also reminds us that a prosperous and secure life is no proof of divine favor. It is not our present security that determines our final destiny. Nor are our sufferings a sign of God's disfavor. God is full of compassion and mercy. He hears our cries and he will answer at the appropriate time and set things right.

The Chinese teach children about the need for patience and endurance by reminding them of the way a Chinese bamboo tree grows. For the first four years, its seed does little, but in the fifth year it may grow to eighty feet tall in just six weeks. The transformation is amazing! Similarly, we may not see

---

35. *The Testament of Job*, 27.7.
36. The word "compassion" refers to a deep emotion, such as a mother's deep affection for her children. In the NT, it is a quality that is often associated with Christ (Matt 9:36; 14:14; 15:32; 20:34; Luke 1:78; 10:33; 15:20; Phil 1:8).

the Lord acting immediately, but when he does, his judgment will be clear, swift, and evident.

5:12 Respecting Solemn Promises

Earlier James spoke of the need to remember God when making business plans (4:13–16); now he speaks of the need for integrity when making business agreements or entering into other commitments. He writes, "Above all, my brothers and sisters, do not swear – not by heaven or by earth or by anything else. All you need to say is a simple 'Yes' or 'No.' Otherwise you will be condemned" (5:12).

This is the last of the many warnings against sins of speech in this letter (see also 1:26; 3:3–12; 4:11; 5:9), which may be why James prefixes it with the words, "above all."[37] Another reason for giving this command such prominence may be that he is quoting Jesus in the Sermon on the Mount: "Do not swear an oath at all: either by heaven, for it is God's throne; or by the earth, for it is his footstool; or by Jerusalem, for it is the city of the Great King. And do not swear by your head, for you cannot make even one hair white or black. All you need to say is simply 'Yes' or 'No'; anything beyond this comes from the evil one" (Matt 5:34–37). Jesus's words can be seen as expanding on the command against misusing God's name in the Ten Commandments (Exod 20:7; see also Lev 19:12).[38] This command accentuates the importance of integrity in speech. Those who are perfectly honest have no need to swear oaths to back up their promises.

In ancient times, many business dealings were done by verbal agreements in which the parties invoked the names of various gods or goddesses as witnesses to their agreement. The thinking was that these gods and goddesses would take revenge on those who violated the contract. The Jews, however, would not swear by pagan gods, nor would they swear by the name of the Lord (since they respected the third commandment: "You shall not misuse the name of the LORD your God" – Exod 20:7). Instead, they swore by heaven or earth, which were metaphorical references to the throne of God or the footstool of God (Isa 66:1; Matt 5:35). This is the context in which James instructs his readers not to swear "by heaven or by earth or by anything else" (5:12a).

---

37. The conjunction *de* at the beginning is more likely to be continuative than adversative (as in NIV, NRSV, NJB).
38. The epilogue begins with an apparent allusion to a saying of Jesus, perhaps deliberately so in highlighting the authority of James's teaching.

Jesus calls his followers to simple honesty and integrity in their speech and actions.[39] Christians' business dealings must be so straightforward that there is no need for oaths or swearing: "A person's 'no' should be adequate to convey his unmitigated denial or disclaimer. His 'yes' should require nothing to enhance its credibility."[40] Any deviation from this simple formula suggests the possibility of fraud. The Latin American scholar Elsa Tamez writes, "If total honesty is achieved in the community, it will not be necessary to swear, for what is said simply and without duplicity will be believed."[41]

James wants Christians to be known for their unqualified truthfulness, total honesty, and uncompromising integrity. Chu Geg Liang, a loyal advisor to a king in China, showed this type of integrity. On his deathbed, the king asked Chu Geg Liang to guard the country and guide the young heir to the throne. When the king died and his son became king, some people urged Chu Geg Liang to take the throne away from the son. But Chu Geg Liang refused. He had promised to help the young king, and he would continue to do so, even at great personal cost. He was a man of true integrity. Christians should be no less committed to being loyal to Christ and known for their personal integrity.

James's closing words on this topic are: "Otherwise you will be condemned" (5:12b). Here he reflects the Lord's words: "I tell you that everyone will have to give account on the day of judgment for every empty word they have spoken. For by your words you will be acquitted, and by your words you will be condemned" (Matt 12:36–37). If Christians make promises that they do not intend to keep, they will be judged for that.

Chinese believers have a regular reminder of these truths each time they write the Chinese character for "honesty" 誠. It is a combination of the characters signifying "speech" and "fulfillment." In other words, honesty is doing what one says one will do. Similarly, the character "trust" 信 combines the concepts for "human being" and "speech," implying that one's speech should be trustworthy. When the Chinese characters for "honesty" and "trust" are combined, they form the character "integrity" 誠信, signaling that when one's promises are fulfilled, integrity is achieved. A Chinese saying makes the

---

39. For Scripture's emphasis on integrity, see L. Cheung, "Integrity," in *Dictionary of Scripture and Ethics*, eds. J. B. Green et al. (Grand Rapids: Baker Academic, 2011), 411–413.
40. William R. Baker, *Personal Speech Ethics in the Epistle of James*, WUNT 2, no. 68 (Tubingen: Mohr, 1995), 280.
41. Elsa Tamez, *The Scandalous Message of James: Faith without Works Is Dead*, trans J. Eagleson (New York: Crossroad, 1992), 56.

same point: "A promise kept is worth a thousand pieces of gold. It didn't need swearing on heavens and gods to back it up."

James wants his readers to speak the truth and act with integrity since they represent the Lord Jesus Christ. His words still apply to us in Asia today – our words must be truthful and our promises trustworthy. That way, no one will need to ask us to swear by God, and the name of the Lord Jesus will not be marred by our insincerity and falsehoods.

5:13–18 Restoring People

James alluded to prayer in chapter 1 when he said, "If any of you lacks wisdom, you should ask God [i.e., pray to God], who gives generously to all without finding fault, and it will be given to you" (1:5). Now he expands his teaching on prayer: "Is anyone among you in trouble? Let them pray. Is anyone happy? Let them sing songs of praise. Is anyone among you sick? Let them call the elders of the church to pray over them and anoint them with oil in the name of the Lord" (5:13–14).[42]

James knows that life can be hard and that troubles will come. Thus Christians should pray, asking not only for wisdom when facing trials (1:5), but also for help when they are suffering hardship. This help may come either in the form of deliverance from their difficulties or strength to endure, as was often the case with the prophets.[43] Even the Lord Jesus prayed when he faced the suffering of the cross, and he was strengthened, though not delivered from the ordeal that lay ahead (Matt 26:39, 42; Heb 5:7).

James knows that there are also happy times in life – times when we are with close friends, or celebrating a wedding or the birth of a baby. At such times, we should "sing songs of praise" (5:13b), expressing gratitude to God for his goodness (Judg 5:3; Pss 7:18; 9:3; 32:2; Eph 5:19). Those in the congregation who are happy or cheerful because of God's blessings should feel free to rejoice and praise.

Sickness is also a fact of life, and is common in contexts of poverty, where some lack food, clothing, and shelter (2:15). So, James gives instructions on what to do when someone is ill: "Is anyone among you sick? Let them call the elders of the church to pray over them and anoint them with oil in the name

---

42. Some interpret this as a chiastic structure in which the first and third scenarios address the same topic of prayer (A–B–A). Another interpretation is that the first two scenarios refer to general conditions whereas the last one refers to a specific type of suffering.

43. The verb "suffer hardship" (*kakopatheō*) is a cognate of the "suffering" (*kakopathia*) the prophets endured (5:10).

of the Lord" (5:14). James is not saying that Christians should not consult physicians when they are ill, but he is reminding them that sometimes, sickness may be more than just a physical malady.[44] When believers are sick, whether their illness is physical, emotional, or spiritual, they need the compassion and friendship of fellow Christians.

The leaders in the local church should be summoned to pray for the sick person. Note that these "elders" are not faith healers or shamans, who magically cure illnesses; rather they represent the entire congregation (Acts 11:30; 14:23; 1 Tim 4:14; 5:17–19; Titus 1:5–9; 1 Pet 5:1).[45] As such, they visit ailing members of the congregation, pray for them, "and anoint them with oil in the name of the Lord" (5:14b).

In the NT, anointing with oil was associated with happiness and well-being. We can see this from Jesus's words:

> When you fast, do not look somber as the hypocrites do, for they disfigure their faces to show men they are fasting. I tell you the truth, they have received their reward in full. But when you fast, put oil on your head and wash your face, so that it will not be obvious to men that you are fasting, but only to your Father, who is unseen; and your Father, who sees what is done in secret, will reward you. (Matt 6:16–18)

Pouring oil on someone was a way of honoring them (Matt 26:6–7; John 12:3).[46] Similarly, the elders' visit, their anointing, and their prayer would honor and bring happiness to the sick. Their presence would also demonstrate the unity within the congregation, where when one member suffered, others cared for them (1 Cor 12:26). The elders must visit, pray, and anoint "in the name of the Lord," meaning, they go with the authority of the Lord to restore this ailing brother or sister.

---

44. Keith Warrington, "James 5:14–18: Healing Here and Now," *International Review of Mission* 93 (2004): 350–351. The word *ekklēsia* ("church") corresponds to the *qāhāl* ("assembly") of Israel gathered to worship God and to receive instructions and blessings from him (Deut 4:10; 9:10; 18:16; 31:30; 1 Kgs 19:20).

45. John H. Elliott, "Elders as Leaders in 1 Peter and the Early Church," *Currents in Theology and Mission* 28 (2001): 549–559.

46. This oil does not seem to have been for medicinal purposes, unlike in Mark 6:13 and Luke 10:34. For ceremonial use of oil, see Moo, *Letter of James*, 240–242. Some think that the oil was symbolic – encouraging the sick to have faith in God. Gary S. Shogren, "Will God Heal Us? A Re-Examination of James 5:14–16a," *EvQ* 61, no. 2 (1989): 105–106; Daniel R. Hayden, "Calling the Elders to Pray," *BSac* 138 (July 1981): 265.

Imagine a situation where some poor laborer, worn out by constant troubles, has given up and is lying in bed. He or she is physically, emotionally, and
spiritually sick. They have lost any hope of justice. But when the elders come,
pray, and pour the oil of gladness on the sufferer, their prayers "offered in faith
will make the sick person well" (5:15). The elders' prayers help sufferers to
count their blessings (1:2), renew their faith, and help them recover from their
sickness and discouragement. The Lord works through the elders' prayers to
effect healing and salvation, whether physical or spiritual.[47]

The elders' prayer may also bring forgiveness: "If they have sinned, they
will be forgiven" (5:15b). Although not every sickness is due to sin (that was
the mistake made by Job's friends), it is also true that some sickness is a result
of sin. The law said:

> If you do not carefully follow all the words of this law, which
> are written in this book, and do not revere this glorious and
> awesome name – the LORD your God – the LORD will send fear-
> ful plagues on you and your descendants, harsh and prolonged
> disasters, and severe and lingering illnesses. He will bring upon
> you all the diseases of Egypt that you dreaded, and they will
> cling to you. The LORD will also bring on you every kind of
> sickness and disaster not recorded in this Book of the Law, until
> you are destroyed. (Deut 28:58–61)

In the NT, there are a few instances where sin is linked with sickness and death,
for example, the case of Ananias and Sapphira (Acts 5:1–11). Paul says that
improper behavior at the Lord's Supper had resulted in sickness and death
among the Corinthians (1 Cor 11:30). James, too, says that if the one who
was physically sick had committed some sin that was causing them suffering,
and they pray about it with the elders, the Lord will forgive them, and they
will receive spiritual (and possibly physical) healing.[48]

Note that James is not saying that if someone does not recover from
an illness, it is because they lack faith. His point is that when someone is
physically, emotionally, or spiritually ill, the prayerful ministry of the church
elders may restore joy and faith. When faith is rekindled, confession of sin and

---

47. Although the passage speaks of physical deliverance (see also Mark 3:3; 5:41; 10:49;
Luke 7:14; John 11:29), it could include eschatological salvation. Hartin, *James*, 268; Dan
G. McCartney and Robert Yarbrough, *James*, BECNT (Grand Rapids: Baker Academic,
2009), 256.
48. For forgiveness of sin leading to healing, see Lev 5:5; 16:21; Num 5:7; Neh 1:16; 9:2; Job
33:26–30; Prov 20:9; 28:13; Pss 32:5; 38:3–4.

forgiveness follow. The healing is often more than just physical healing; it may be the spiritual healing of restoration to community and fellowship with God.

Confession, forgiveness, and restoration are so important that James says, "Therefore confess your sins to each other and pray for each other so that you may be healed" (5:16a). The present tense verb indicates that this is to be a regular practice. It is also to be mutual, with believers confessing "to each other" and praying "for each other." Perhaps the sins being confessed here are not so much sins against God as much as sins against each other.

When the Lord Jesus Christ was talking about praying for forgiveness (Matt 18:19–20), Peter wanted to know, "Lord, how many times shall I forgive my brother or sister who sins *against me*? Up to seven times?" (Matt 18:21; italics added). The Lord answered, "I tell you, not seven times, but seventy-seven times" (Matt 18:22). Sins against God are confessed to God, and God forgives. But when we sin against each other, we should confess to one another as well as to God and forgive one another, up to seventy-seven times!

James possibly remembers this teaching of the Lord when he asks the elders to meet with ailing believers, hear their confession, confess their own shortcomings, so that there might be physical and spiritual healing within the community.[49] The ailing believer, the elders, and the church would be restored to one another by forgiving one another.

If they have sin against God, they need to repent and change their ways. This type of confession to God before others requires honesty and trust within the group, and it is essential to the wholeness and holiness of the community: "It is in the celebration of our solidarity as broken people in need of healing that compassion is born."[50]

The emphasis on mutual prayer and healing shows that prayer for healing is not the exclusive responsibility of the elders; it is a privilege shared by the entire community. Healing takes place only where people are willing to acknowledge their own weaknesses and bear each other's burdens. The practice of forgiveness and restoration in the power and presence of Christ is essential if we are to have transformed lives and grow to spiritual maturity.

James concludes: "The prayer of a righteous person is powerful and effective" (5:16b). In this context, the "righteous person" is someone who has acknowledged their sin, sought the prayer of the elders, and received divine

---

49. For instances of forgiveness leading to spiritual healing and restoration, see Deut 30:3; Isa 6:10; 53:5; Jer 3:22; Acts 28:27; Heb 12:13; 1 Pet 2:24.
50. James C. Fenhagen, *More Than Wanderers: Spiritual Disciplines for Christian Ministries* (San Francisco: Harper & Row, 1978), 34–35.

spiritual healing. Their prayers are powerful and effective because they are in line with God's desire and wishes. This is true even if the one praying is poor or ill.

James gives an example of an ordinary person with extraordinary power in prayer because he agrees with God's will: "Elijah was a human being, even as we are. He prayed earnestly that it would not rain, and it did not rain on the land for three and a half years. Again he prayed, and the heavens gave rain, and the earth produced its crops" (5:17–18).

James's audience would have revered Elijah: he did miracles (1 Kgs 17:14), prophesied (1 Kgs 21:22), parted the Jordan River (2 Kgs 2:8), brought down fire from heaven to fall on sacrifices or soldiers (1 Kgs 18:38; 2 Kgs 1:10, 12), raised the dead (1 Kgs 17:22), and departed the earth in a fiery chariot (2 Kgs 2:11–12). But James wants his readers to remember that Elijah had the same emotions and drives as every other human being. This great prophet was afraid and gave in to despair when Jezebel vowed to kill him: "Elijah was afraid and ran for his life. . . . He came to a broom bush, sat down under it and prayed that he might die. 'I have had enough, LORD,' he said. 'Take my life; I am no better than my ancestors'" (1 Kgs 19:3–5). He was truly human.

Elijah also believed in YHWH God, which made him a "righteous person" and his prayer effective: "He prayed earnestly that it would not rain, and it did not rain on the land for three and a half years. Again he prayed, and the heavens gave rain" (5:17b–18).[51] James mentions this specific incident from the life of Elijah because it is linked to the theme of repentance. The drought ended and the rains came after the people "fell prostrate and cried, 'The LORD – he is God! The LORD – he is God!'" (1 Kgs 18:38). When the people confessed their sin, Elijah prayed, and it rained again and "the earth produced its crops" (5:18b).[52] Similarly, when believers – also merely human – pray together, confessing their sins, there will be healing and restoration.

James had another reason for citing Elijah, namely that there was a famous account of Elijah healing by prayer:

> Some time later the son of the woman who owned the house be-
> came ill. He grew worse and worse, and finally stopped breath-
> ing. She said to Elijah, "What do you have against me, man of

---

51. The difference between the OT account of three years (1 Kgs 18:1) and James's three-and-a-half years can be explained as an approximation.
52. There is an allusion here to the example of a farmer patiently waiting for the autumn and spring rains (5:7).

God? Did you come to remind me of my sin and kill my son?" "Give me your son," Elijah replied. He took him from her arms, carried him to the upper room where he was staying, and laid him on his bed. Then he cried out to the LORD, "LORD my God, have you brought tragedy even on this widow I am staying with, by causing her son to die?" Then he stretched himself out on the boy three times and cried out to the LORD, "LORD my God, let this boy's life return to him!" The LORD heard Elijah's cry, and the boy's life returned to him, and he lived. Elijah picked up the child and carried him down from the room into the house. He gave him to his mother and said, "Look, your son is alive!" Then the woman said to Elijah, "Now I know that you are a man of God and that the word of the LORD from your mouth is the truth." (1 Kgs 17:17–24)

Similarly, believers' prayers can be effective and bring healing. Elijah was a mere human; yet, he was a believer and so his prayers were powerful and effective.

ELDERS AND PRAYER

As a former lay-elder for over twenty years, I take to heart my responsibilities as an under-shepherd (1 Pet 5:1–4) and strive to be readily available when parishioners heed James's admonition to call on the elders of the church to intercede for them.

Too often elders so emphasize their oversight of church personnel and operations that they have little time and energy to spare for the pastoral care of members. But anointing the sick with oil implies going to visit members. Remote prayers cannot replace personal presence. Being with people who are suffering affirms that they are important and assures them that they are not forgotten. The elders incarnate Christ's presence.

Jesus's own ministry showcased the importance of personal presence and touch. He visited Jairus's home to resurrect his daughter (Luke 8:41–56) and went to the centurion's home to resurrect his son (Luke 7:6b–10). He touched and healed a leper (Matt 8:2–3) and a woman with a disabling spirit (Luke 13:11–13). In each instance, Jesus's presence and his touch offered tangible evidence of the value he placed on people. We as elders should do likewise in going to our people wherever they are. Our presence and our prayers minister powerfully.

Yet reality imposes limits on our availability. We have full-time jobs, family responsibilities, and the oversight of the church. How can we respond to every request for visitation? We cannot, and so each church needs to have a number of elders so that responsibilities can be shared and tasks delegated.

The initiative rests with the one who is in need. They may pray for themselves (Jas 5:13) or they may call on their elders to intercede for them (Jas 5:14). How are they to decide which course of action to take? The answer may lie in the exact words James uses.

James advises those "in trouble" to pray for themselves. The Greek word translated "trouble" occurs only three other times in the New Testament. Paul uses it twice to refer to religious persecution (2 Tim 2:9; 4:5) and James used it earlier to exhort his readers to steadfastness by citing the example of Old Testament prophets who suffered patiently (Jas 5:10). So "trouble" in James 5:13 probably refers to religious persecution or suffering that comes because of one's service to Christ. Christians are to expect and accept such sufferings, and pray for strength to remain faithful (Jas 5:11).

On the other hand, when believers face "sickness" (Jas 5:14), they are to call the elders to pray. The word used for sickness, *astheneo*, covers a wide range of meanings: physical illness (Mark 6:56; Luke 4:40), limitations of one's faith (Rom 4:19; 14:1–2; 15:1), vulnerability of one's conscience (1 Cor 8:7, 9–12; 9:22), spiritual deficiency of the unsaved (Rom 5:6), relative immaturity of believers (Rom 6:19), inferior social status or influence (1 Cor 1:25, 27; 2:3; 4:10), vulnerability to temptation (Heb 4:15), and the inherent limitations of being human (Heb 5:2; 7:28). So, if James is using this word to connote situations of an inadequate faith or vulnerability to temptation, clearly such believers need the elders to stand with them to support them in their struggles, strengthen their faith, and safeguard them from Satan's attacks.

The elders do this by praying for and anointing the one who is suffering with oil. Although the parable of the Good Samaritan depicts oil as having medicinal value (Luke 10:34), it was predominantly a symbol of divine blessings or favor (Pss 23:5; 45:7; 89:20; 92:10; 104:15; 133:2; 141:5). The elders communicate God's favor by anointing the sick with oil. God will respond to their intercession according to his will.

Culturally, we may not pour oil on people today. But we can find ways to indicate God's favor by offering words of encouragement and assurance. If sick persons confess their sins, we can offer them reconciliation and lead them to the true high priest, the Lord Jesus Christ.

We can assure them that we will stand by them in their time of crisis. God's power flows through the elders' prayers, bringing healing and restoration – physically, emotionally, or spiritually.

Gilbert Soo Hoo

5:19–20 Rescuing Sinners

James concludes his letter with a call to rescue sinful souls. In the preceding passage (5:13–18), he explained how to restore an ailing believer. Now, he explains the blessing of restoring a believer who has wandered away from truth because of sin.

Once again, he addresses his readers as, "my brothers and sisters," and says, "If one of you should wander from the truth and someone should bring that person back, remember this: Whoever turns a sinner from the error of their way will save them from death and cover over a multitude of sins" (5:19–20). The phrase, "one of you," stresses the mutual responsibility of the community toward this wandering person.[53] This person has wandered from the truth by yielding to desires and falling into sin (1:14–15) or has been deceived into committing sin (1:16). Either way, the person is no longer within the congregation. He or she is still a Christian, but is no longer within the congregation and its fellowship. To be alone is dangerous, and may even lead to spiritual death (5:20b). That's why the church should intervene to restore such a person. James encourages them to do this, reminding them that "whoever turns a sinner from the error of their way will save them from death and cover over a multitude of sins."[54] The faith community should encourage and support such efforts to reach out to save wanderers.

James's words about sins being covered recall the proverb: "Hatred stirs up conflict, but love covers over all wrongs" (Prov 10:12; see also 1 Pet 4:8).[55] Although only God can forgive sin (Ps 32:1), the community's effort to restore

---

53. This is the third time in this chapter that James uses the phrase *among you* (5:12, 13; see also 1:5; 2:16; 3:13; 4:1).

54. The verb "turn back" refers to Israel turning back to God (Isa 6:10; Jer 3:12; Ezek 18:30–32; Hos 3:5).

55. In the Greek OT, the wording of this proverb is different from James and Peter, possibly because they were quoting it from memory or because they are quoting different traditions (Johnson, *The Letter of James*, 339).

a wandering person may lead them to the place where they are ready to repent of those sins and draw near to God.

In our world, which is full of hatred, violence, uncertainties, distractions, temptations, trials, and differing moral codes, young – and even mature – believers often wander from the truth. We should all be concerned about the souls of such troubled people. God wants us to be mediators between life and death. By our acts of kindness and goodness, we can deliver many from a hopeless eternity. Blessed are those who reach out to them and restore them to faith and to the believing community.

The abrupt ending of the letter, with no benediction or goodbye, seems odd. Nevertheless, the letter of James has taught us many important and powerful lessons. And we do well if we heed James's own exhortation: "Do not merely listen to the word, and so deceive yourselves. Do what it says" (1:22).

May God find us faithful!

SELECTED BIBLIOGRAPHY

Adamson, James B. *The Epistle of James*. NICNT. Grand Rapids: Eerdmans, 1976.

Allison, Dale C. *James*. ICC. London: Bloomsbury, 2013.

Andria, Solomon. "James." In *Africa Bible Commentary*, edited by Tokunboh Adeyemo. Grand Rapids: Zondervan, 2006.

Baker, William R. *Personal Speech Ethics in the Epistle of James*. WUNT 2.68. Tubingen: Mohr, 1995.

Batten, Alicia. "God in the Letter of James: Patron or Benefactor?" *New Testament Studies* 50 (2004): 257–272.

Bauckham, Richard J. "James." In ECB, edited by James D. G. Dunn and John Rogerson. Grand Rapids: Eerdmans, 2003.

_____. "The Tongue Set on Fire by Hell [James 3:6]." In *The Fate of the Dead: Studies on the Jewish and Christian Apocalypses*, 119–131. Leiden: Brill, 1998.

Blomberg, Craig L. and Mariam J. Kamell. *James*. ZECNT, edited by Clinton E. Arnold. Grand Rapids: Zondervan, 2008.

Byron, John. "Living in the Shadow of Cain: Echoes of a Developing Tradition in James 5:1–6." *Novum Testamentum* 48, no. 3 (2006): 261–274.

Cheung, Luke L. *The Genre, Composition and Hermeneutics of James*. Carlisle: Paternoster, 2003.

_____. "Integrity." In *Dictionary of Scripture and Ethics*. Edited by Joel Green. Grand Rapids: Baker Academic, 2011.

Davids, Peter H. *James*. NIGTC. Grand Rapids: Eerdmans, 1982.

Davis, George B. "Preaching from the Book of James." *Criswell Theological Review* 1 (1986): 137–147.

Dibelius, M. *A Commentary on the Epistle of James*. Translated by M. A. Williams. Hermeneia. Philadelphia: Fortress, 1976.

Felder, Cain Hope. "Partiality and God's Law: An Exegesis of James 2:1–13." *The Journal of Religious Thought* 39, no. 2 (1982): 51–69.

Fung, Robert Y. K. "Justification in the Epistle of James." In *Right with God: Justification in the Bible and the World*, edited by D. A. Carson. Grand Rapids: Baker, 1992.

Hiebert, E. Edmond. *James*. Chicago: Moody Press, 1992.

Hort, Fenton J. A. *The Epistle of St. James*. London: Macmillan, 1909.

Isaacs, Marie E. "Suffering in the Lives of Christians: James 1:2–19A." *Review & Expositor* 97, no. 2 (2000): 183–193.

James, Arthur. "James." In *South Asia Bible Commentary*. Udaipur, India: Open Door Publications, 2015.

Johnson, Luke. *The Letter of James*. AYBC. New York: Doubleday, 1995.

Laws, Sophie. *The Epistle of James*. Peabody, MA: Hendrickson, 1980.

Marcus, Joel. "'The Twelve Tribes in the Diaspora' (James 1.1)." *New Testament Studies* 60, no. 4 (2014): 433–447.

Martin, Ralph P. *James*. WBC. Waco: Word, 1988.

Maynard-Reid, Pedrito U. *Poverty and Wealth in James*. Maryknoll: Orbis, 1987.

McKnight, Scot. *The Letter of James*. NICNT. Grand Rapids: Eerdmans, 2011.

Mitton, C. L. *The Epistle of James*. London: Marshall, Morgan & Scott, 1966.

Moo, Douglas J. *The Letter of James*. PNTC. Grand Rapids: Eerdmans, 2000.

Ropes, James H. *Epistle of St. James*. ICC. Edinburgh: T & T Clark, 1916.

Sawicki, Marianne. "Person or Practice? Judging in James and in Paul." In *The Mission of James, Peter, and Paul: Tensions in Early Christianity*, edited by Bruce D. Chilton and Craig Evans. Leiden: Brill, 2005.

Tamez, Elsa. *The Scandalous Message of James: Faith without Works Is Dead*. Translated by J. Eagleson. New York: Crossroad, 1992.

Tillman, William M. "Social Justice in the Epistle of James." *Review & Expositor* 108 (2011): 417–427.

Wall, Robert W. *Community of the Wise: The Letter of James*. NTC. Valley Forge: Trinity Press International, 1997.

Ward, Roy Bowen. "Partiality in the Assembly: James 2:2–4." *Harvard Theological Review* 62, no. 1 (1969): 87–97.

Wolmarans, Johannes L. P. "Misogyny as a Meme: The Legacy of James 1:12-18." *Acta Patristica et Byzantina* 17 (2006): 349–361.

Yarbrough, Robert. *James*. BECNT. Grand Rapids: Baker Academic, 2009.

Asia Theological Association

54 Scout Madriñan St. Quezon City 1103, Philippines
Email: ataasia@gmail.com Telefax: (632) 410 0312

OUR MISSION

The Asia Theological Association (ATA) is a body of theological institutions, committed to evangelical faith and scholarship, networking together to serve the Church in equipping the people of God for the mission of the Lord Jesus Christ.

OUR COMMITMENT

The ATA is committed to serving its members in the development of evangelical, biblical theology by strengthening interaction, enhancing scholarship, promoting academic excellence, fostering spiritual and ministerial formation and mobilizing resources to fulfill God's global mission within diverse Asian cultures.

OUR TASK

Affirming our mission and commitment, ATA seeks to:

- **Strengthen** interaction through inter-institutional fellowship and programs, regional and continental activities, faculty and student exchange programs.
- **Enhance** scholarship through consultations, workshops, seminars, publications, and research fellowships.
- **Promote** academic excellence through accreditation standards, faculty and curriculum development.
- **Foster** spiritual and ministerial formation by providing mentor models, encouraging the development of ministerial skills and a Christian ethos.
- **Mobilize** resources through library development, information technology and infra-structural development.

To learn more about ATA, visit www.ataasia.com or facebook.com/AsiaTheologicalAssociation

Langham
PARTNERSHIP

Langham Literature, with its publishing work, is a ministry of Langham Partnership.

Langham Partnership is a global fellowship working in pursuit of the vision God entrusted to its founder John Stott –

> *to facilitate the growth of the church in maturity and Christ-likeness through raising the standards of biblical preaching and teaching.*

Our vision is to see churches in the majority world equipped for mission and growing to maturity in Christ through the ministry of pastors and leaders who believe, teach and live by the Word of God.

Our mission is to strengthen the ministry of the Word of God through:
- nurturing national movements for biblical preaching
- fostering the creation and distribution of evangelical literature
- enhancing evangelical theological education

especially in countries where churches are under-resourced.

Our ministry

Langham Preaching partners with national leaders to nurture indigenous biblical preaching movements for pastors and lay preachers all around the world. With the support of a team of trainers from many countries, a multi-level programme of seminars provides practical training, and is followed by a programme for training local facilitators. Local preachers' groups and national and regional networks ensure continuity and ongoing development, seeking to build vigorous movements committed to Bible exposition.

Langham Literature provides majority world preachers, scholars and seminary libraries with evangelical books and electronic resources through publishing and distribution, grants and discounts. The programme also fosters the creation of indigenous evangelical books in many languages, through writer's grants, strengthening local evangelical publishing houses, and investment in major regional literature projects, such as one volume Bible commentaries like the *Africa Bible Commentary* and the *South Asia Bible Commentary*.

Langham Scholars provides financial support for evangelical doctoral students from the majority world so that, when they return home, they may train pastors and other Christian leaders with sound, biblical and theological teaching. This programme equips those who equip others. Langham Scholars also works in partnership with majority world seminaries in strengthening evangelical theological education. A growing number of Langham Scholars study in high quality doctoral programmes in the majority world itself. As well as teaching the next generation of pastors, graduated Langham Scholars exercise significant influence through their writing and leadership.

To learn more about Langham Partnership and the work we do visit **langham.org**

www.ingramcontent.com/pod-product-compliance
Lightning Source LLC
Chambersburg PA
CBHW071813090426
42737CB00012B/2074

* 9 7 8 1 7 8 3 6 8 8 6 6 1 *